D0758235

THE ORIGINS
AND RISE OF
ETHOLOGY

THE ORIGINS AND RISE OF ETHOLOGY

The science of the natural behaviour of animals

W. H. Thorpe

Heinemann Educational Books

PRAEGER SPECIAL STUDIES • PRAEGER SCIENTIFIC

Published in Great Britain in 1979 by
Heinemann Educational Books Ltd
22 Bedford Square, London WC1B 3HH

LONDON EDINBURGH MELBOURNE AUCKLAND
HONG KONG SINGAPORE KUALA LUMPUR NEW DELHI
IBADAN LUSAKA NAIROBI JOHANNESBURG
EXETER (NH) KINGSTON PORT OF SPAIN

ISBN 0 435 62441 5

Published in the United States and Canada in 1979
by Praeger Publishers
A Division of Holt, Rinehart and Winston/CBS, Inc.
383 Madison Avenue, New York, New York 10017 U.S.A.
Praeger Pub. No. 9 056 987654321
ISBN: 0–03–053251–1

Library Cataloguing in Publication Data

Thorpe, William Homan
    The origins and rise of ethology.
    1. Animals, Habits and behavior of
    2. Ethologists
    591.5   QL751
    ISBN 0–435–62441–5 (UK)
    ISBN 0–03–053251–1 (USA)

Printed and bound in Great Britain by
Morrison & Gibb Ltd, London and Edinburgh

Contents

Introduction   vii

Part I: The Origins of Ethology

1   The early history of natural history   3
2   The earliest origins of ethology   9
3   The British contribution to the development of ethology: through the nineteenth into the twentieth century   18
4   Ethology in the United States of America 1880–1940   36
5   The establishment of ethology in continental Europe (1910–50)   53

Part II: The Rise of Ethology

6   The conceptual system at 1950: key topics and attitudes   87
7   New post-war research groups and laboratories   108
8   The present position of ethological concepts and research   126
Postface: ethology—what of the future?   165
Index   171

Acknowledgements

I have received assistance and encouragement from a number of friends and colleagues in the preparation of this book. The project commenced as a result of the invitation of The Association for the Study of Animal Behaviour to give the first Niko Tinbergen Memorial Lecture and I am indebted to the Officers for being willing to forgo the immediate publication of the lecture in their journal in favour of my making it the basis of a book. Edward Armstrong capped fifty-five years of friendship by providing some valuable comments and by reading the galley proofs during what turned out, alas, to be the last weeks of his life. Priscilla Barrett drew a number of the illustrations and Miss Gillian Edwards compiled the index.

Dr Katharina Heinroth kindly supplied the photograph of Oskar Heinroth and Dr Hans Lissmann that of Jakob von Uexküll. He also gave me some vivid personal reminiscences of the latter's qualities both as a teacher and an investigator.

To the Royal Society and the British Psychological Association I am indebted for permission to reproduce photographs from their journals.

W.H.T.

Introduction

The distinguishing characteristics of ethology and the nature of the ethological approach will be discussed in more detail in later chapters of this book, but in this introduction it seems desirable to make a brief preliminary statement about the differences between the two main disciplines which were developed to study and interpret the behaviour of the whole intact animal organism—in contrast to the working of its parts which is of course mainly the task of the physiologist. These two disciplines are psychology and ethology.

Psychology originally implied the study of the mind, but during the last century or so it has come more and more to signify the study of an individual's actions, behaviour, and responses. Since one cannot directly study the mind, all one can do is to ask the individual subject to reveal his mental processes as the basis of his responses and his choices—in short, to explain his reasons for doing things. Hence, in psychology one is not investigating the mind directly, but is enquiring into the subject's interpretation of his own mind.

But psychology did not concern itself solely with human beings for long. By the 1880s many psychologists were becoming 'comparative', interested in studying the differences between the behavioural abilities of man and at least the higher animals. This was an important development; but even so psychologists as a whole still remained anchored to the idea that their main task was to investigate the behaviour of man, and primarily as the expression of his psyche. Thus they have always tended to look at man as the paradigm and to compare the performance and abilities of animals with his.

The fundamental change in attitude of behavioural scientists resulted from the advent of the theory of Evolution by Natural Selection. This implied the adoption of a truly comparative approach to the different types of animal life; not primarily comparing them with human beings, but one with another, starting at the lower or lowest levels with such organisms as the protozoa and the echinoderms; and then working successively upwards to other animal groups. This was done almost entirely by zoologists who, because of Darwin's basic work, have always been particularly devoted to evolutionary explanations. So it was natural for them to commence by examining similarities in patterns of behaviour (as, for example, the distinctive mode of scratching or preening in birds), similarities which are not necessarily correlated with the specific structure of the species but might be regarded as expressions of evolutionary relationships. In other words, the zoologist is always enquiring how different animals and different animal groups have achieved the same ultimate aims of developing, finding food and the other necessities of life, and reproducing successfully, in such a fantastic variety of ways. This also implies that the zoologist is always interested in the niceties of adaptation—whether of locomotory organs, sense organs of every kind, or reproductive methods, etc.—as related to the particular environment in which the animals are living.

So there are obvious reasons why ethology, which we can for the moment define as 'the comparative study of the natural behaviour of animal species', has arisen from zoology and was, in its earlier developments, almost entirely pursued by zoologists.

It is remarkable that when ethologists and comparative psychologists start to talk to one another they almost always miss each others' points! The ethologist is always asking (a) how it has come about that the animal can do this or that; (b) what the selective pressures which necessitated these developments and maintain them once established are; and (c) why it is that a relatively simple animal like a starfish and a relatively complex one like an octopus

have both successfully maintained themselves, in similar environments, with only minor changes, through vast periods of geo-
logical time. The comparative psychologist, on the other hand, is
usually not thinking about these at all. For a very long time he was
concerned with understanding the 'intelligence' of animals as
compared with the 'intelligence' of man, and so he tended to carry
out experiments offering choices between particular stimuli or
particular patterns of behaviour in what were, for the animal,
highly artificial conditions. And he was doing this long before he
had much valid information about the sense organs and sensory
abilities of the species concerned. The result was that his comparisons between the behaviour of animals and men were often
highly spurious, since he was asking the animal quite inappropriate
questions by exposing it to experimental situations (puzzle boxes,
mazes, choice-chambers, etc.) which it could not possibly 'understand', and so asking it 'questions' so far removed from its ordinary
environment that only by lucky chance could it be expected to
yield reasonable or meaningful answers. As we shall see, both
ethology and comparative psychology have developed greatly and
come much closer together in recent years. But there is still this
hard core difference, and if we do not realise its existence and do
not understand its origins, we may encounter much confusion
and misunderstanding.

It was Charles Darwin who, with his studies of instinct, and
with his last book *The Expression of the Emotions in Man and
Animals*, showed the way forward. But (as explained in a later
chapter) there were reasons why the impact of this profound work
upon students of behaviour in general was slow in manifesting
itself.

It is of great importance to remember that, because of its
earliest objectives and its desire to make comparisons between
mental abilities and performances, psychology tended to treat
animals as if they were tiny men and so was subjective in approach.
It is true that psychology, as it became more comparative, began
to sense the danger of the subjective and strove to achieve greater
objectivity. On the other hand, as soon as ethology became an
organised discipline it stressed the importance of 'objectivity'.

This implied the need to know, as exactly as possible, the environmental characteristics to which the animal was adapted, the kind of situation in which it had to achieve a successful response, and the means available to it of making these responses. It was immediately realised that as complete an inventory as possible must be made of the whole repertoire of actions available to the animal in its normal environment; and such special techniques as were developed by the early ethologists were primarily those which aid and make more precise this basic observation: the technique of keeping animals under observation yet with the minimum of interference; the technique of marking individuals so that they can be recognised throughout long stretches of their lives; and the techniques which aid the recording of their consequent actions and behaviour. Ethology is thus essentially a naturalist's approach and so it first emphasized and brought under experimental study stereotyped, relatively rigid species-characteristic actions (e.g. the elaborate sexual displays of many species of birds, the web-spinning of spiders, or the nest-building of solitary and social wasps). During these studies ethologists inevitably began to probe problems of causation and so became deeply involved with both causes and functions. Indeed, it is characteristic of ethology today that it always combines the two and so provides developmental and evolutionary explanations.[1] In this combination lies its great strength and promise. Again by way of contrast, psychologists, whether or not they merit the label 'comparative', have traditionally ignored such instinctive behaviour since, centred as they have been on man whose innate behaviour is at a minimum and who has learned responses to almost everything, they have usually assumed when experimenting on the learning and conditioning of animals that 'instinctive' responses and innately pre-formed behaviour can be ignored, and the naïve animal treated experimentally as a *tabula rasa* on which learned responses can be inscribed, confident that no previous behavioural tendencies exist which may influence or render nugatory their results.

As a final word to this introduction one should emphasize that, although this alternative between 'subjective' and 'objective' has been significant in the story, it can nowadays be over-stressed. Obviously science always needs to be objective. Yet when we are studying living animals, which are in some degree, however slightly, similar to ourselves, it is always salutary to attempt to put ourselves in the animal's place in our imagination, and consider what we should do in similar circumstances. If we have started out by being sufficiently objective in our observations and experiments to learn enough about the animal's sensory equipment and, in short, its 'world', then a 'subjective' attitude can be of great value in designing better subsequent experiments and in knowing how to evaluate the animal's behaviour. In other words, the closer the initial rapport a behavioural biologist can establish with the animal he is studying the more successful his investigations are likely to be. And it is no accident that, as will become clear during the course of this book, a majority of the great ethologists were pet-keepers in their early youth.

REFERENCES

1. Tinbergen, N., 'On aims and methods of ethology', Z. Tierpsychol., 1963, 20, 410–33.

In memory of
Edward Allworth Armstrong
1899–1978

Part I

THE ORIGINS OF ETHOLOGY

I

The early history of natural history

Ecology started with natural history, as did so much else in biology, and one may regard ethology and ecology as the modern scientific versions of the two main aspects of natural history; the rival term 'bionomics' (coined by Ernst Haeckel) found slight favour and seems now to have withered away.

It has long been realised that the origin and development of the attitude of mind which led western man to observe animal life objectively, to depict animals accurately, and to describe them precisely was a slow process. There are remarkably vivid pictures of animals in prehistoric cave sites, many of which manifest exact observation. Such representations are believed to have had magico-religious significance. But, for example, an engraving of nesting snowy owls (*Nyctea scandiaca*) is notable as indicating interested observation.[1] In historic times the Egyptians portrayed some birds vividly, including three species of goose, some birds of prey, domesticated ostriches (*Struthio camelus*) and cranes (*Grus grus*) being force-fed. They also depicted wild-fowling scenes. The Greeks, notably Aristotle, and the Romans to a lesser extent, made desultory notes on the behaviour of animals. A number of species are mentioned in the Greek Anthology.[2]

Some vivid paintings of birds can be seen, including a third-century picture of a passerine feeding chicks at the nest. A few of the early Fathers of the Church had a real feeling for nature and we hear of a monk spending most of the day observing ants; but birds such as the eagle, dove, and peacock were important religious symbols. Religious and social conditions were such that little study was devoted to natural history. Birds and other animals were thought of in anecdotal, moralistic terms such as had been represented earlier in Aesop's *Fables*.

Until animals were correctly depicted and described, exact classification was impossible and description of behaviour retarded, and until this epoch was reached it was difficult to make objective natural history observations. But, in the thirteenth century, coinciding with the activities of St Francis of Assisi (1181–1226), a highly significant change in the attitude to Nature occurred. It does not seem excessive to claim that this change initiated, or made possible, the whole development of biology.[3]

In the same century, the writings of St Albertus Magnus and the Holy Roman Emperor Frederick II show the beginnings of some reasonably accurate observation of natural history. But, apart from birds, progress was still remarkably slow. However, recent studies of illuminated manuscripts, particularly the devotional works known as 'Books of Hours' which were written and illuminated for the heads of great families like Charles the Noble, the Duc de Berry, Catherine of Cleeves, etc.,[4] have shown how, from the late thirteenth century through the fourteenth and fifteenth centuries, the marginal illustrations of these works began to display not only recognisable birds (which can occasionally be found much earlier) but also recognisable *species* of insects (butterflies, moths, bugs, dragon-flies, etc.) and, later, molluscs. These exquisite works of art seem to show clearly the gradual growth of accurate observation of nature.

So the recognition of a few animal species was well on the way by the fifteenth century. And in the sixteenth century Gesner, Aldrovandi, and Turner were giving effective descriptions of a variety of animals, although often still incorporating fantastic imaginative details and even describing entirely imaginary beasts. Real enlightenment did not come to western Europe until the seventeenth century when John Ray in this country and Baron von Pernau in Germany initiated a movement with which all students of natural history are familiar.[5] Ray's achievement was so outstanding that we must say a little more about him.

John Ray was the son of an Essex blacksmith who entered

Catharine Hall, Cambridge, in 1644, and two years later, at the age of nineteen, transferred to Trinity College. Here his outstanding ability resulted in a fellowship in 1649 and appointment to lectureships in Greek, Humanities, and Mathematics, and also to a variety of college offices. He started to study botany in 1650 and after ten years' intensive field work produced his study of the plants of the Cambridge area, and then in due course his *Catalogus Plantarum Angliae et Insularum Adjacentium* (1670). He had decided that his life work lay in the university when, with but little warning, the Act of Uniformity which demanded assent to everything in the Anglican Prayer Book, presented him with a plain issue of conscience. For a man of his clear sighted integrity there was only one course—so in August 1662 he found himself (as did 2000 other clergy) at the age of thirty-five, his vocation clear but his life work hardly begun, cut off from the University and from all prospect of employment, and forced to take a private tutorship in the country. His friend Willughby saved the situation, and the years 1660–72 were filled with journeys, often in Willughby's company, to explore every corner of England, and included three years intensive travel and study in Europe. Raven claims (it seems with full justice) that these years of travel were comparable in effect to the voyage of the Beagle in Darwin's story.

The death of Willughby in 1672 left him without a co-author for his projected *Systema Naturae* and apparently with little means except the £60 annuity provided by Willughby's will. The following year he married and the remaining thirty-three years of his life became a period of stupendous output, without secretary or assistance, from the seclusion of his little home at Black Notley, near Braintree in Essex.

Ray's greatest work is probably his *Historia Plantarum* (1686–88) which gives ample indication of his genius as a taxonomist. He was able to fasten unerringly upon the essential characteristics of a species and his active and critical mind was impelled by a vivid appreciation of the beauty of all living things as part of their natural environment. And it was Ray's principles which much later made possible the development of systematics in accordance with evolutionary ideas.

As a zoologist Ray, with the publication of Willughby's *Ornithologia* (London, 1676) founded the scientific study of birds. With his *Historia Piscium* (1713) and *Synopsis Quadripedum* (1693) he went far towards doing the same for fishes, reptiles, and mammals. The *Historia Insectorum* was begun late in life, and when he realised the immensity of the task he relinquished all hope of living to complete it. Yet even in this field he showed himself far ahead of his time in recognising the vital taxonomic importance of the study of larval stages as well as adult, and hence of metamorphosis. He of course made mistakes which often seem grotesque to a modern zoologist, but here, as in other connexions, his lack of a microscope and the pioneering nature of even the simplest observation at that time must be held in mind.

Besides his outstanding achievements in taxonomy, Ray displays views on instinct, consciousness, and intelligence which are not unworthy of a present day comparative psychologist, and it is only in the light of recent developments in endocrinology that the full significance of some of his observations on, for instance, the nesting of birds and the control of clutch size, have become apparent. It is interesting to recall his attitude to a number of the current beliefs of his day. He was a spirited advocate of the views of Copernicus and Galileo. He rejected the belief in magic and the supernatural, he denied the reliability of the evidence for spontaneous generation, and in his repudiation of alchemy and transmutation as early as 1660 he was far ahead of Newton. On theological grounds he started with the prevailing assumption that the number of species was pre-ordained by divine authority; yet he came to have doubts as to the fixity of species and to champion the view that fossils were the remains of living organisms, and not due 'to any kind of plastik virtue inherent in the earth'. He understood the true nature of the sedimentary rocks and realised the significance of these facts for the prevailing doctrines for the 'novity of the world'. Raven argues, I believe justly, that by his profound work, *The Wisdom of God Manifested in the Works of Creation* (1691) he 'gave to the development of science a status and sanction of the highest value; and so far as Britain is concerned, freed it from conflict with ecclesiastical authority until it had become an established element in the national character. His own honest and reverent mind, fearless in facing facts but slow to dogmatise prematurely, or to reject established opinion until the evidence was clear, commended the new philosophy and encouraged less adventurous churchmen to support its claims. When Bishop Butler (1692–1752) expounded the implications of Ray's work in his *Analogy*, when John Wesley made its message a part of his philosophy, when Gilbert White gave it world-wide fame in one of the most popular of English prose classics, he demonstrated that the church was ready to abandon its medieval *Weltanschaung* and re-assert its faith in the worth of the works of the Lord. In consequence in Britain there was a century and a half of scientific progress undisturbed by theological controversies and fostered by the spokesmen of religion. During that time if applied science and the industrial revolution aroused occasional outbreaks of revolt against the machine, the love of birds and flowers, the desire to understand nature as well as to admire her products, and the discovery in such activity of rich recreational, educative and religious opportunities became a national characteristic.'

To give one further example of the seminal nature of some of Ray's observations on behaviour we may mention that he records the example of a swallow which, as a result of the experimenter's daily abstraction of an egg, laid a total clutch of nineteen before deserting, and says 'another experiment I shall add to prove that though birds have not an exact power of numbering, yet have they of distinguishing many from few, and knowing when they come near to a certain number: and that is that when they have laid such a number of eggs as they can conveniently cover and hatch they give-over and begin to sit: not because they are necessarily determined to such a number, for they are not, as is clear, because they have an ability to go on and to lay more at their pleasure . . . This holds not only in the domestic and mansuete [tame] birds, for them it might be thought to be the effect of circulation [regular repetition] and institution [early training], but also in the wild.'

Again on the subject of instinctive behaviour Ray writes, 'birds of the same kind make their nests of the same materials, laid in the same order and exactly in the same figure, so that by the sight of the nest one may certainly know what bird it belongs to: and this they do though they never saw, nor could see, any nest made, that is though taken out of the nest and brought up by hand.' It is remarkable and by no means to the credit of modern ornithology that about three centuries passed before there was much careful observation and experiment on this subject. Ray was also acquainted with, and saw the significance of, the early records of territory in birds—though he added nothing in this field himself. Coming to anatomy, it is remarkable to find him regularly dissecting birds as early as 1658 and describing the 'labyrinth' found on the trachea of many male ducks, the function of which is still by no means clear. He understood the action of the woodpecker's tongue, and many other beautiful adaptations besides.

Much more could be added; but enough has been said to show that, for the historian of science, his work constitutes a landmark indeed and that every naturalist—whether his interest be plants, birds, fishes, mammals, or insects—will find in it a great store of thought-provoking observation and of interesting early records, giving delightfully vivid glimpses of the wild-life of Britain and of many parts of Europe in the seventeenth century. More perhaps than any other naturalist of his period, he laid the first foundations of the future sciences of ethology and ecology.

REFERENCES

1. Armstrong, E. A., *The Folklore of Birds* (London: Collins, 1970).
2. Raven, C. E. (1942 and 1947) and Thompson, D'A. W., *A Glossary of Greek Birds* (1895, 1936).
3. Armstrong, E. A., *Saint Francis: Nature Mystic* (Berkeley: University of California Press, 1973).
4. Hutchinson, G. E., *American Scientist*, 1974, 161–71 (and others).
5. Raven, C. E., *John Ray Naturalist: his life and works* (Cambridge: CUP, 1942); *English Naturalists from Nekham to Ray: a study of the making of the modern world* (Cambridge: CUP, 1947).

2

The earliest origins
of ethology

When did ethology start and whence did it come? The answer is quite clear—it first appeared in France in the late eighteenth and early nineteenth centuries. In fact, ethology made at least three somewhat unpropitious starts each of which, however, ultimately played a part in its full establishment.

But first let us look at the origin of the word 'ethology'. In the seventeenth century an actor or mimic who portrayed a person's character was regarded as a practitioner of ethology and called an ethologist. This usage lapsed in the eighteenth century when the term was employed to signify the science of ethics.

In the nineteenth century John Stuart Mill[1] developed the name ethology to cover the 'science of building character' whilst employing the term 'psychology' for the science of the 'elementary laws of mind'. He said, 'if we employ the name psychology for the science of the elementary law of mind, ethology will serve to denote the science which determines the kind of character produced in conformities of those general laws, by any set of circumstances, physical and moral. According to this definition, ethology is the science which corresponds to the act of education, in the widest sense of the term, including the formation of national or collective character, as well as individual.' All of this was of course quite outside the perview of the zoologists who were clearly the mainspring of what was to become ethology: psychology as a science was not yet 'invented'.[2]

The earliest seed of ethology in our present-day sense germinated in France. And the man who tended the growth of the first seed was no 'scientist' but of much humbler status: yet we now see him as a figure of great significance. He was C. G. Leroy (1723–89), a man of high intelligence and excellent education (though 'merely' a nobleman's gamekeeper) who studied animal behaviour as part of his work. His book, *The Intelligence and Affectability of Animals from a Philosophic Point of View, with a few letters on Man*, was published in France in 1764 and must surely have been known to all the participants in the Paris discussions (to be described below) but unfortunately did not become widely known in England until over a century later, when an English translation appeared.[3]

Both the book and the man are so extraordinary that any modern account of the history of behaviour studies should surely contain a paragraph or two about them. Charles Georges Leroy succeeded his father as ranger of Versailles and Marly. In this post he enjoyed ample opportunity for the observation of animals and took the fullest advantage of the situation. He was a friend of Diderot, d'Alembert, and Helvétius; he contributed to the *Dictionary of the Encyclopaedia* and lived a quiet life throughout. His French editor described him as 'a faithful friend; gentle, kind, and firm to his subordinates, he bore himself worthily, and even loftily, towards his superiors and those who claimed to be so by birth.' In view of his friendship with leading *philosophes* and representatives of the enlightenment, his sturdy independence of mind as, for example, in his anti-mechanistic views noted below is still more remarkable.

His book is entirely in the form of letters addressed to a lady, Madame d'Angiviller, with whom he was intimate. I have not succeeded in finding out anything about her, but the book is prefaced by a dedicatory letter to Madame ******** elaborating the fantasy that the work is not by himself but that the lady has asked him for the letters of 'The Naturalist of Nuremberg' on animals and men. He proceeds to say that he has had much difficulty in meeting with this little work, now become rare; but at last has the pleasure of sending it to his patron. He then explains that he has added a few of his own to the letters of 'The Naturalist'. He continues to remark that he, Leroy, holds that none but a sportsman can fully appreciate the intelligence of animals and that to know them thoroughly you must have associated with them; and at this point most philosophers fail. He asserts that this Nuremberg Naturalist is, or was, 'like myself a determined sportsman and went to his course of philosophy in the woods.' He continues, 'I agree with him in thinking that in the study of animals, isolated facts must be put aside. It is their daily conduct, the whole of their acts, with their modifications according to circumstances, all working towards the objects which they must necessarily have in view, each according to its nature, that constitutes the true field of observation.'

After this he points out that he will only deal with animals which we have constantly under our eyes and which we can follow in all their proceedings, and that even amongst these we should choose those with which we have some affinity, either in structure or habits. Insects, for instance, he regards as far too much removed from the sphere of our observation for us to be able to follow their operations in detail. By contrast he says 'the republic of rabbits, the association of wolves, the precautions and characteristic wiles of foxes, the sagacity shown by dogs in their various reactions with us—all these are far more instructive than the industry of bees on which so much stress is laid."

Proceeding to his first 'letter' we find immediately a remarkable link with the modern ethologist. 'For instance I should like to have the complete biography of every animal. I should wish that after its individual character, natural appetites, and way of life had been treated of, the observer should endeavour to see it in all the circumstances which may arise to oppose the immediate satisfaction of its wants—circumstances whose varying nature breaks the regularity of its ordinary proceedings, and forces it to have recourse to fresh devices.' In other words Leroy is demanding what we now call an 'ethogram' for each species!

Following out this programme Letter II deals with Fox and Wolf. Letter III compares carnivores with herbivores, e.g. deer, hare, and rabbit, whereupon there follows a discussion of instinct *versus* sensibility. He gives it as his view that a system of automatism is both obscure and dangerous and asks whether it is not more natural and at the same time more satisfactory to consider sensibility 'as generally diffused throughout the whole animal kingdom, exercising itself in different degrees and under an infinite variety of forms in harmony with the wants which excite each individual into action and with the organisation which sets the limit to each species?' He then says '. . . shall we give the preference to the arguments of a false philosophy, which teaches us to look upon these beings as acting without motives for action, and simply swayed by blind impulses? . . . I prefer to observe each individual set in motion by sensibility, obeying his own peculiar affections, and thus contributing to the perfection of the whole and the just proportion which should reign between the species. I am struck with the same spectacle in the order of society; and surely the persuasion of a general and diffused sensibility makes the spectacle still more grand and I give myself up the more readily to this idea because we have seen how much trouble and how many unintelligible and gratuitious suppositions the contrary opinion will cost us.'

In many places in the book he gives long arguments for criticising the theory that animals are automata—particularly when he is comparing the behaviour of wild and domestic animals. He has a particularly charming section in Letter IV which I can briefly summarize:

'We have often read together, Madame, the excellent histories that M. de Buffon has given us of many of the animals. We have admired the eloquence of this great naturalist. The sagacity with which he seizes the characters which distinguish each species shows the truth of his pictures, and his brilliant colouring. In giving an account of those animals which he had himself observed, or of which he had before him reliable accounts, the details of their inclinations and actions, of their sagacity, and of their skill, are painted with an exactness and a charm which make him far outstrip all his predecessors. As long as he keeps the thread of observation in his hand, his path is sure: he penetrates the intentions of the animals, and, by his manner of describing their actions, lays open all their movements to the reader with the skill of a master.

'But could we have supposed it? The author of the histories of the deer, the dog, the fox, the beaver, the elephant, appears wholly to disregard facts when he comes to argue; he then becomes one of the great detractors from the intelligence of animals. Doubtless he has more right than his fellows to look upon his own as a species apart, but, after all, being man, he is fallible, and we must be allowed the right of testing his opinions, provided it be done with the respect due to his person, and to his eminent talents.'

Leroy, being impatient of philosophy, held that although we can never understand the nature of the mind of animals, this does not matter. What is important is the increase in our self-knowledge which results from studying the behaviour of animals. As Gray remarks,[4] Leroy was the spiritual founder of the comparative analysis of behaviour, in Europe. And looking at the writings of some who followed him in France one cannot help feeling that Leroy was more fully in possession of the ideas which now sustain ethology. I agree with Gray when he says that 'Leroy would have been at home in any of our modern behaviour laboratories', though I would have emphasized his peculiar ethological quality. Indeed there are few pages of his book which do not provide us with stimulating insights into animal behaviour and charming glimpses of the character of its author—and perhaps too of the lady to whom it was addressed!

The next phase in the development of ethology in France depends on Lamarck (1744–1829) who produced his *Zoological Philosophy* in 1809. Our almost automatic reaction today to the name Lamarck is summed up in the phrase 'the inheritance of acquired characters'. At the time the accepted view was that animals represented separate creations, assumed to have taken place after one or more catastrophic destructions of floras and faunas by natural disasters.

The most significant fact about Lamarck was his denial of 'special creation' and his emphasis on the fact of evolution (*transformisme*). He regarded evolution as being brought about by the inherited effects of use and disuse; and this, so he thought, was the result of the animal striving to achieve new goals and occupy new niches. By emphasizing this 'striving' he was bringing forward one of the basic problems of ethology—that of the 'internal drive', its nature and origin.

Lamarck's views on 'inheritance', though largely dismissed by later biologists, seemed natural and reasonable to most of his contemporaries, for David Hume (1711–76) held it to be self-evident that the beasts, as brothers of men, were endowed with thought and reason. It is worth quoting Hume's expression of this, 'we are conscious that we ourselves, in adapting means to ends, are guided by reason and design, and that it is not ignorantly nor casually we perform these actions which tend to self preservation, to obtaining pleasure and avoiding pain. When therefore we see other creatures, in billions of instances, perform like actions, and direct them to like ends, all our principles of reason and probability carry with us an invincible force to believe the existence of a life cause.'[5] But when Lamarck introduced this concept of *transformisme* into the minds of zoologists there was a tremendous reaction from the zoological establishment represented (in his case) by the great Baron Georges Cuvier of Paris.

Cuvier assumed that there must have been innumerable catastrophic inundations but that they were not universal phenomena so did not affect the entire surface of the globe. Thus when the waters receded the new dry lands were repopulated from former areas which had been safe from the flooding. In this way he was able to hold on to the doctrine of one special creation by the Almighty.

The first entry of ethology, in our present sense, into the European scientific hierarchy grew out of the famous debates around 1830 in the Académie des Sciences in Paris. The proponent of ethology in this case was Étienne Geoffroy-Saint-Hilaire (1772–1844) who took up the cause of Lamarckism against his colleague Cuvier,[6] who completely dominated French biology at that time. As Julian Jaynes says,[7] 'he was the great apostle of the immutability of species . . . and therefore of comparative anatomy which was then the study of the inter-relationships of these created beings.' His influence as head of the Académie and the most famous scientist of his time was huge and suffocating; effectively keeping those thinking along different lines out of high scientific positions. Étienne Geoffroy-Saint-Hilaire was the brilliant early evolutionist whose central concept was the unity of plan of composition throughout all animal species. But Étienne, like Lamarck, was a somewhat meek individual, and whereas Cuvier's emphasis was always on laboratory-discovered facts, that of Étienne was on the Lamarckian trends as they are found in nature, which, as we have seen, were considered to be the result of the conscious strivings of the animals themselves. This led to a tremendous confrontation in which the naturalistic evolutionary point of view of Étienne was smothered by the suffocating weight and authority of his former colleague. As Jaynes says, 'Étienne was right in principle though weak in his facts; Cuvier was right in his facts but wrong in principle.'

So, in a sense, it was Lamarck who made animal psychology and ethology attractive by stressing the drive or striving of the animal as a factor in the adaptation of species; and the debates of 1830 hastened the firm establishment of both comparative psychology and ethology. Certainly in these debates the position defended by Étienne was Lamarckian and presupposed much from Leroy. Though he did not himself go into great detail he particularly stressed the essentials as set forth by Leroy of what was to become ethology. But alas the building crumbled under Cuvier's attack and so seems to have been demolished almost before it rose from the ground.

However Étienne's failure was not a complete disaster and the topic was soon revived. Cuvier died in 1832 but on his deathbed (so to speak) he persuaded the Académie des Sciences to appoint his protégé Flourens to the post of 'perpetual secretary'. Flourens was perhaps pre-eminent as the effective founder of the modern study of the physiology of the brain. He was led into this course through his horror and revulsion at the so-called science of phrenology, which was running wild in Europe as the result of the activities of F. J. Gall, a German who was propagating his ideas in Vienna. Flourens, as a result of his brain operations on pigeons, was in fact regarded as one of the founders of comparative psychology; though once in his secure and lifelong appointment his mental powers rapidly fossilized!

Étienne Geoffroy-Saint-Hilaire survived Cuvier for twelve years but there seems to have been no more fight left in him. Fortunately he had a son, Isidore, who kept his father's views alive and between the years 1854 and 1864 produced his great *Histoire Naturelle Générale*. In the last of the three volumes of this work he in effect re-founded ethology and used that word in virtually its present-day meaning (which was also that of Leroy and Étienne) but also including some of what we now call ecology. We can regard this as the second or the third European 'foundation' of ethology, according to taste. But even this foundation was far from successful for, sound naturalist though he was, Isidore had no outstanding academic position and many saw him as merely flogging the dead horse which his father Étienne had sponsored. So once again the climate of opinion was unfavourable—and this time exacerbated by the writings of a truculent German, Ernst Haeckel, who had just coined the term 'oecology' to denote the study of the organism in its environment. Haeckel was another aggressive type who tended to dominate all opposition: a scientific popularizer of evolution whose extreme materialistic cosmology, with its sweeping but shaky conclusions, impressed the materialistic rationalists of the late nineteenth century but is little regarded today.

To complicate matters, the term 'ethology' was still in use in England in the sense of John Stuart Mill; so confusion became worse confounded, some people mistaking ecology for ethology and some *vice versa*, and in both cases not being quite sure what was meant by either term!

However, even then, all was not lost; for Isidore Geoffroy-Saint-Hilaire passed the torch of his vision of the need for ethology as a constituent of the biological science of the future to a fine all-round French naturalist, marine biologist, and Professor at the Sorbonne, Alfred Giard (1846–1908). The latter was effective in founding two or more marine biological stations in France. He was an evolutionist, still of a somewhat Lamarckian type (and so tending to place natural selection in a secondary role), who, as a result of his great experience of marine invertebrate life, saw clearly the need for both ethology and ecology. So he (together with the great entomologist J.-H. Fabre (1823–1915)) kept the concept of ethology alive in Europe and on into the present century, thus ushering us into the modern period.

Here we must leave continental Europe for the time being to look elsewhere—only to find yet other attempts at the foundation of ethology. We will finally return to Europe for what may be called the climax of the story.

REFERENCES

1. Mill, J. S., *A System of Logic* (1843).
2. Wilhelm Wundt (1832–1920) is usually regarded as the first psychologist. His two key books were *Lehrbuch des Physiologie des Menschen* (Heidelberg, 1864) and *Handbuch des medicinischen Physik* (Berlin, 1867).
3. Leroy, C. G., *The Intelligence and Affectability of Animals from a Philosophic Point of View, with a Few Letters on Man* (London: Chapman and Hall, 1870).
4. Gray, P. H., *Early Animal Behaviourists: Prolegomenon to Ethology* (*Isis*: **59,** 372–83, 1968).
5. Quoted by Gray, op. cit., from Hume, D., *A Treatise of Human Nature* (London: John Noon, 1783).
6. Coleman, W., *George Cuvier: Zoologist* (Cambridge, Massachusetts: Harvard University Press, 1964).
7. Jaynes, J., 'The historical origins of "ethology" and "comparative psychology",' *Animal Behaviour*, 1969, **17,** 601–6.

3

The British contribution to the development of ethology: through the nineteenth into the twentieth century

As was made clear in Chapter 1, Great Britain had not been behind the continent in the development of natural history to the point at which the behaviour of animals was ready to become a major issue. The eighteenth century saw a great development in good and reliable natural history and by the end of that period Daines Barrington (1727–1800), Thomas Pennant (1726–98), T. Bewick (1753–1828), Gilbert White (1720–93), T. Montague (1751–1815), and others were laying the foundations of scientific ornithology.

In 1872 the real pioneer appeared in the person of a young man called Douglas Spalding, who in that year published in *Nature* a paper on instinct followed by six other papers relating instinct to the acquisition of behaviour through experience; the last appearing in 1875, the year of his death from tuberculosis. Spalding's first paper thus antedated most of the important writing on animal behaviour produced in England in the nineteenth century.

Spalding was born in London about 1840 of working class parents. He worked as a slater in Aberdeen, educated himself, and attended Professor Baines' lectures on psychology. In 1872 he read the above-mentioned paper to the British Association. The importance of this paper was at once realised and it appears to have been as a result of this that Lord Amberley, a noted free-thinker, appointed him tutor to his sons, one of whom was the future Bertrand Earl Russell. The Amberleys cooperated with Spalding in the experiments carried out on the estates of their family seat at Ravenscroft in which he first showed that hand-reared swallows kept in cages too small to permit flying, flew 'perfectly' on the first opportunity. Lord Amberley, who died in 1876, left provision in his will that Spalding was to continue as tutor to his sons. However, as the result of a legal action which attracted considerable attention at the time, the provision of this will was set aside by a court of law and the children were educated in the faith and practice of the Church of England. However Spalding was not, as is sometimes said, tutor to Bertrand Russell who was at that time too young, but to his elder brother who turned out to be a fine scion of the Russell stock. J. B. S. Haldane (1954) argues that had Spalding lived a few more years, 'even if only to the age of fifty, there can be little doubt that he would now be recognised as the principal founder of what is now called ethology.'

Spalding was in effect neglected by many of us until Haldane re-introduced and published his work in 1954. This is extra-ordinary since Spalding's studies eventually inspired Lloyd Morgan to become an animal experimenter himself. I confess that though I, as a young man, had read the major works of Lloyd Morgan, I equally had neglected Spalding and was astonished and stimulated by Haldane's re-discovery!

Spalding's interest was apparently first aroused by controversies attending Bishop Berkeley's theory of perceptual learning, which proposed that the discrimination of objects in space could not be due to vision only but must include correlated kinesthetic sensory experiences. Berkeley's theory had been hotly debated since its publication in 1709 but it was Samuel Bailey's 1842 critique of Berkeley which was Spalding's particular inspiration. (Gray points out that Spalding, being a very well-read man, must surely have known of the further criticism of Berkeley by T. K. Abbott which appeared in 1864.) Spalding wisely chose to undertake experiments on the domestic chick, for, as others had pointed out before, the behaviour of the chicks at and after hatching shows itself too quickly to be merely the result of experience.

Spalding's influence on research into the development of behaviour is not an easy topic because, as P. H. Gray shows in a most useful study,[1] during his life at Ravenscroft with the Amberley family, Spalding had a considerable collection of animals available for study though little ready opportunity to publish his observations. In those days of course there were no journals devoted to the publication of this kind of matter (apart from *Nature*). There were however the scientific societies such as the Linnean Society, the Zoological Society of London, and the Royal Society, but these were closed except to members or 'fellows' and Spalding did not belong to any of them. The British Association for the Advancement of Science was open to anyone who wished to attend and speak, and it is clear that Spalding read several papers at British Association Meetings, but most of them appear not to have been published. So it was that, apart from the first paper on instinct,[2] his main article was published in *Macmillan's Magazine* of 1873, and entitled 'Instinct, with original observations on young animals'.[3] This was naturally not a publication where the author could give a great deal of scientific detail, it had to be of interest to the average general reader and to offer such facts as would be likely particularly to interest the magazine's clientele.

The next difficulty is that Spalding was not particularly interested in what we should now speak of as animal learning, then known as 'problem solving'. This was, in part at least, because naturalists had by that time generally accepted the conclusion of David Hume's *A Treatise of Human Nature*[4] that higher animals use the same principles of intelligence that man uses. So why waste time on giving further examples of this when everybody agreed with it anyway? Much more important to the British scientists of the period was the problem of instinct, and it was this problem that, from the behavioural point of view, assumed the central place in *The Origin of Species* and in *A Posthumous Essay on Instinct* by Charles Darwin which G. J. Romanes included in his *Mental Evolution in Animals* (London, 1884). In fact in his essay in *Macmillan's Magazine*, Spalding wrote 'before passing to the theory of instinct, it may be worthy to remark that, unlooked for, I met with in the course of experiments some very suggestive, but not yet sufficiently observed phenomena: which however, have led me to the opinion that not only do the animals learn, they can also forget—and that very soon—that which they never practise.' Gray suggests very plausibly that this implies that Spalding had intended to study learning much more thoroughly when he had finished his observations on instinct.

In our century a student of behaviour would, in all probability, commence a study of the theories of visual and auditory perception by ignoring the latter and testing visual perception by isolating the subject in a dark room. Spalding proceeded differently. First, in order to control the experience of the chick and to guarantee that the experience would be known to the experimenter, Spalding hatched the eggs himself. He did this, long before the era of incubators, by suspending them in a cloth slung above a kettle of steaming water!—the first known artificial incubator used in the study of animal behaviour. Then to control the experience of the subject after hatching, it was necessary that the functioning of eyes and ears be prevented. Modern experimenters would have used some method of occluding these organs. Spalding knew that it is not necessary for the chick to eat during the first few days of life until the food supply of the yolk is exhausted and the chick's eyes are still closed, when, before lung respiration is commenced, it breaks through to the air-sac at the large end of the egg. At this point therefore there has obviously been no experience of patterned vision. So Spalding opened the eggs at the air sac, drew out the head and literally unwound it and attached a small translucent hood, fixed with an elastic band, over the head. As long as the chick is given some help in divesting itself of its shell (which Spalding did) it will survive well enough.[5]

Spalding hatched other chicks in a dark bag. In order to control auditory experience, he sealed the ears of some unhatched chicks with gummed paper and allowed them to serve as their own controls. Those which responded to the sound of the hen, calling from her confinement in a wooden box, *before* the gum was removed, were taken from the experiment. In Spalding's work only three chicks passed the control test; but when the gum was removed from the ears of these three, they, like the others, ran straight to the auditory target. As Gray says, Spalding either did not conduct or did not report on a further control experiment, since it is possible that the chicks would have performed similarly to a source of any sound. But that they did perform and that they ran in the correct direction was however a suitable test for Spalding's objective at the time since the nineteenth-century psychologists applied Berkeley's theory of perception to humans and animals alike. And in a further experiment with the hen in a box, Spalding took the chicks which had been reared in a dark bag when they were several days old and placed them singly about ten feet from the box—with the result that all went straight to the target! He says 'nine chickens were thus experimented upon, and each individual gave the same positive result, running to the box scores of times, and from every possible position.' But Spalding also noted (a point confirmed by Gray's experiments) that the chicks seldom took a step forward by themselves when they were hooded. They did however walk backwards so that such a chick looked like a cat trying to withdraw its head from a paper sack; but of course the cat will have had experience whereas the chick had always had its head restricted—first in the egg and then in the hood.

Spalding also made observations on audition which were equally astonishing. Twenty chicks were kept hooded for several days; some of these were then released individually in a yard in the presence of a hen. After a few minutes of standing motionless the chick would go straight to the adult animal, encountering little if any difficulty with the terrain. 'It never required to knock its head against a stone to discover that "there was no road that way".'[6] He also at this time made observations on the maturation of pecking and carried out studies of pigs separated from their mother at birth—showing that they would also perform to the sounds of the mother. As Gray remarks, 'The sum influence of these experiments on visual and auditory development can be seen in the extensive literature [e.g. on 'releasers' and similar topics] which came into being as answer and counteranswer to the problems Spalding initiated.'[7]

Thus it is not surprising to find that the releaser concept of modern ethology was in some degree anticipated by Spalding. Believing that instinct and learning go hand in hand in the same species and individual, he naturally came to the conclusion that, at least in a great many cases, the function of instinct is to guide the course of learning and is not a complete substitute for it. This was all part of his insistence that when comparing animal with human behaviour, and indeed when comparing the behaviour of different species of animal, we can easily make absurd mistakes if we do not allow for the fact that different species are born in different developmental stages. From this it follows that we should not directly compare a new-born chick with a new-born human infant since the latter is born at an earlier stage of development. So he was generally of the opinion that students of animal psychology should endeavour to observe the unfolding of the powers of their subjects in as nearly as possible the ordinary circumstances of their lives.

This all ties in, of course, with his interest in the embryology of behaviour. In this respect he refuted a number of common misconceptions about the hatching process of the chick—including one which had been sponsored by no less a person than Helmholtz who believed that the chick pecks while still in the shell, and on being hatched pecks about at random until it happens to strike a piece of grain![8] Spalding pointed out that the domestic chick cannot peck in the shell because of its cramped position; and that even on hatching it does not peck at first. He also cites Spencer as having put forward the directly opposite view to Helmholtz, believing that the newly hatched chick starts running around immediately, picking up fragments of food. Spalding argued that such a chick can no more do this than a new-born child can run about and gather blackberries! In his article in *Macmillan's Magazine* (1873) Spalding gives quite an accurate description of the way in which the chick rotates its upper body in the shell and cuts its way out by means of a horny rasp on the top of its beak. This is not pecking. After the hatching, the wet, bedraggled and nearly helpless chick needs a few hours to develop muscular functioning.

Thus it was that Spalding, in his few years of activity, produced results which impinged on the nature of instinct, the release of instinctive actions, the embryology of behaviour, the maturation of behavioural function and, above all, on 'imprinting'. So although he was for a while neglected, if not actually forgotten, he has a reasonable claim to be yet another 'founder of ethology', having given rise to the flow of activity which developed in this country throughout the next seventy years.

Following Spalding the subject received an immense stimulus from the work first of Romanes but much more importantly of Lloyd Morgan. Not only was his work studied intensively and some of it repeated by Lloyd Morgan; R. H. Lewis in *Problems of Life and Mind* (1873-79) cited his unpublished observations of a gosling reared away from water, which refused to enter a pond when first taken to one at the age of some months. Later J. B. Watson upbraided Spalding for not having done exactly this; but he had failed to read William James' *Principles of Psychology* (1890) where it is recounted.

It is interesting to note that 1872 was the date of the first publication of Darwin's *The Expression of the Emotions in Man and Animals*, a work which had a tremendous influence on the development of the study of animal behaviour, in that here was an outstandingly original *comparative* study of behaviour, a true pioneering achievement. It is however a curious fact that this influence was long delayed, not reaching its true proportions until the present century; this is perhaps to be explained by the over-riding importance of Darwin's previous work for biological science in general: it almost seems as if the scientific community was overwhelmed by the problems which Charles Darwin had raised and so felt, at the time, incapable of seriously undertaking anything further! Be this as it may, Spalding's work received much recognition for a period of ten or fifteen years after his death, and it did so primarily because of the writings of Lloyd Morgan, who surely must have been attracted by Spalding's experimental (rather than comparative and observational) approach, which was outstanding for the period. It is, however, remarkable that the immediate stimulus which brought about Lloyd Morgan's entry into animal psychology was neither Spalding nor Darwin, but a disagreement with Romanes. G. J. Romanes (1848–94) was a zoologist of great attainments, a close friend of Darwin, and one of the first who rallied to his standard. Moreover he was one of the pioneers in invertebrate physiology and his work in this field was highly valued in his day (see particularly his work on echinoderms).

Romanes' first major work, entitled *Animal Intelligence*, was eventually published in 1882. It was the first general treatise on 'comparative psychology' to be written and its author believed that the subject would come to rank alongside that of comparative anatomy in importance. Romanes did not deal directly with the problem of mental continuity between animals and man but, as E. G. Boring said,[9] he was content to present the great mass of data on animal behaviour, thus laying the groundwork for a subsequent argument on the relation of animals to men. He obtained his material, as indeed did Darwin, from an exhaustive combing of both the scientific and popular accounts of animal behaviour, a procedure which subsequently became somewhat unfairly known as 'the anecdotal method'. Romanes tried to be rigorously selective in choosing his examples, but in fact his work savoured far too much of the highly credulous writings of early nineteenth-century naturalists (good examples of which are W. Bingleys' *Animal Biography* (1829), and J. Couch's *Illustration of Instinct* (1847)). It was this credulity and anecdotage that raised Lloyd Morgan's ire to the point at which he opened the argument in 1884, organizing his attack around the questions of the possibility of a true science of comparative psychology, the definition of instinct, and the question of the nature of consciousness. We need not follow the fortunes of this battle here; it has been well discussed by P. H. Gray.[10] From our point of view the main importance was not only that it led Morgan into comparative psychology and the study of the animal mind and instinct, it was also a factor inducing him to undertake animal experimentation himself.

Lloyd Morgan's contribution was indeed so outstanding as to warrant our considering him as one of the founding fathers of both comparative psychology and ethology. He wrote fourteen substantial books and we can do little more here than indicate very briefly the variety of topics which he illuminated and advanced by his studies.[11] First, he had valuable points to make on the relations between the subjective and the objective approach. In short, he indicates that both are essential to the scientific method (*Introd. Comp. Psychol.*, 1894). Then he investigated the nature *versus* nurture problem, concluding (in opposition to Wundt) that from a biological point of view one should restrict the term 'instinctive' to what is, to a greater or lesser degree, congenitally determined. In this he strongly supported the view that instinct is fundamentally species-specific behaviour (*Habit and Instinct*, 1896). As to the evolution of behaviour, his advice was 'stick to observation and leave theorizing about the *process* of evolution to "armchair philosophers" ' (*Life, Mind and Spirit*, 1925). This was remarkable when we consider that his basic approach was that of a philosopher. He stressed the need for operational definitions, that is, he emphasized the importance of stating definitions specifically, and if possible operationally, since lack of such care can lead to misinterpretation and misconception (*Habit and Instinct*, 1896). He invented the term 'trial and error' as applied to learning, although for a while he spoke of 'trial and failure' and 'trial and practice'; he also made original observations on the behaviour of dogs and it was upon these that his conclusions, set out in *Animal Behaviour* (1900) and *The Animal Mind* (1930), were based. It is clear, I think, that Thorndike was stimulated to begin his own work on cats as a result of hearing Lloyd Morgan's 'Lowell Lectures' in Boston in 1896. In the former book Lloyd Morgan criticizes Thorndike because of the artificiality of his experiments and I do not think Thorndike (*Animal Intelligence*, 1911) took much notice of these comments. Lloyd Morgan also stressed the need, now obvious to us, for replication; he himself replicated a

Figure 1 Conway Lloyd Morgan. Photo by kind permission of
the *British Journal of Psychology*.

number of Spalding's experiments (*Habit and Instinct*, 1896).
He was much concerned with the problem of imitation, implying
by this what we now often label 'observational learning'. In this
respect his work was particularly important in that he held the
concept of instinctively governed restraints or predispositions
which led to the restriction of observational learning to particular
objects and situations (*Habit and Instinct*, 1896; *Animal Behaviour*,
1900). He stressed the importance of the cognitive approach in

which he includes 'association by contiguity' and 'association by similarity' (*Introd. Comp. Psychol.*, 1894, p. 96). Morgan did not, as far as I am aware, actually use the term 'the Law of Effect', but he had clearly the same idea in his 1894 paper. He used and advocated the term 'conditioning' in 1925 (*Life, Mind and Spirit*, p. 108). Incidentally Pavlov's work was first translated into English by Anrep in 1927. Morgan strongly emphasized the virtues of the physiological approach; an emphasis which was first shown in his book of 1894 and was extended in *Instinct and Experience* (1912). In the first of these two works, he said that 'within the cells, during life, chemical changes of a special and complicated nature take place; and associated with these chemical changes there are transformations of energy, of great delicacy and complexity'. Morgan displayed a particular interest in mental phenomena, a concern which derived from his own basic inclinations and his interest in Spalding's work discussed above. In 1894 he anticipated a great deal of our present-day interest by producing original ideas on migration, nest building, and incubation. He made what were probably the first observations on social distance (*Habit and Instinct*, 1896). It is worth noting that he saw the experimental importance of providing a surrogate mother, basing this on the account provided by A. R. Wallace (*Malay Archipelago*, 1896) of making an artificial mother for an orphaned orang-utang baby from a buffalo skin. This was made up into a bundle so that the young animal could always find some hair to cling to (Adler, 1973). Finally, the conclusion with which his name has ever since been associated, known as Lloyd Morgan's canon, must be mentioned. It is important to quote his own words about this (*Introd. Comp. Psychol.*, 1894), 'in no case may we interpret an action as the outcome of the exercise of a higher psychical faculty, if it can be interpreted as the outcome of the exercise of one which stands lower in the psychological scale.' The importance of this has been enormous. It was devised to avoid the biased interpretation resulting from the anecdotal style of writing prior to his time. It is obviously still valuable although nowadays it requires great care in its application. It can lead, for instance, to an extreme reductionist approach to animal behaviour which may assume the existence of a clearly definable physiological interpretation when, in fact, no such interpretation is as yet in sight. It can also lead to extraordinary circumlocutions in an attempt to avoid the implication of mental factors in animal behaviour. Indeed, to the modern ethologist dealing with higher animals and faced as he is with ever-increasing evidence for the complexity of perceptual organization, I feel inclined to say that the very reverse of Morgan's canon often proves to be the best strategy—as indeed not a few psychologists of the American school have now come to stress.[12]

I suspect I am the only active ethologist now alive who actually remembers Lloyd Morgan. Lloyd Morgan spent the greater part of his life teaching at Bristol where he nurtured the University College through to its full University status from the year 1883 until 1919. He became its first Vice-Chancellor, was Professor of both Zoology and Geology, and taught much else besides. He could be a superb lecturer and was an almost compulsive teacher. A friend records how he found him on Clifton Downs lecturing, apparently to whoever wished to stop and listen, on the unlikely subject of coral atolls! After retiring from Bristol he came to live in Hastings, which was then my home town, and was a striking figure about the place, the most impressive feature being his white beard, which in retrospect seems to have been a yard long! (Perhaps my recollection is actually correct. For one of his pupils at Bristol describes him as cycling about the city without an overcoat in any weather and with his long beard resting on the handlebars or blowing wildly over his shoulder!)

I only met Lloyd Morgan at all closely on one occasion and that was indeed memorable for me in that it was in 1927 when I was reading my first scientific paper in public. I was both uplifted and somewhat apprehensive to find that the other two speakers sharing the platform were Lloyd Morgan, who gave a critical evaluation of Eliot Howard's work on territory in bird life, and Professor E. W. McBride, from the Imperial College of Science in London, a great embryologist and zoologist, who was an indefatigable proponent of Lamarckism. Both speakers were orotund and impressive. McBride was a pugnacious Ulsterman who took sides on any subject with virulent intensity. One phrase has stuck in my mind, 'I have yet to see the Mendelian mutation which is not pathological!'.

With Lloyd Morgan we have, of course, entered the modern period but there are one or two of his later contemporaries who deserve mention at this point.

These were chiefly amateurs—which is not surprising since nearly the whole development of ornithology and a great part of the development of entomology in Great Britain during the nineteenth century and early twentieth century was in the hands of the amateurs. That ornithology particularly had been brought to the point of appreciating and understanding the need for a more precise and detailed study of behaviour was due to the most original worker in this field, Edmund Selous (1858–1934). He was a strange figure and perhaps the first ornithologist of note to devote himself, with extreme tenacity of purpose, simply to observing and noting down with great thoroughness exactly what birds were doing in the field when undisturbed. His central aim throughout was to gather evidence for the possibility of the evolution of habits by natural selection. He was an uncompromising and contentious man, a brother of the great hunter-naturalist Frederick C. Selous; and perhaps the wild independence of the African big game hunter had its counterpart in that of the solitary wanderer of the British fields, shores, and hills. Edmund Selous published six books and a mass of miscellaneous notes and records covering the first thirty-five years of the twentieth century. He was particularly interested in the evolution of habit in birds and was a man of real originality of thought. But his style of writing was at times so extraordinary as to be scarcely bearable except by his greatest devotees. It was alternately discursive and then extremely concentrated; elsewhere its unwieldliness and spate of parentheses made it almost unreadable. Yet, though at times bewilderingly intricate and congested it will suddenly change to appear, as H. J. Massingham put it, at best, exhilaratingly, magnificently eloquent, with something of the rugged beauty of a Doughty.*

Here he is discussing the evidence for the origin of parental care for young birds (from *Evolution of Habit in Birds*, 1933).

* C. M. Doughty, author of *Travels in Arabian Deserta*.

'That the force here considered has anything to do with that which binds the parent bird to its offspring, during the earlier period of the latter's existence, may be difficult or even impossible to show, since more generally convincing causes—such, for instance, as that it is "natural" or "deeply implanted"—will always be there to obscure it, at least, if not to make it, through merger, seem wholly unnecessary. I will therefore confine myself to giving some extracts from what is as yet and will, I fear, continue to be the last of my field diaries, showing, according to my own sense of evidence, that it is there and plays its part at a stage of these relations which, if so, makes it a matter of extreme probability that it does so throughout. I consider the here-following observations, taken together with those of a more spectacular, but like, nature, to be of immense importance or significance (or something of that class), because they seem to me to present some possible evidence of there being, in organic nature generally, irrespective of Man (who does strut so) a finer essence behind the totality of that coarsely material cosmos which, with evil, pain and grief inherent in it, should present itself, in so far as its supposed highest product—human existence—is concerned, as something even more abhorred in the imagination than

> "a tale
> told by an idiot, full of sound and fury,
> signifying nothing."

'For, surely, a sort of Super-Nero or Ivan the Super-terrible, a *Grandiose* Peter, Alexander, Napoleon, etc., etc., telling *his* tales, however awful, by *making* them (for this is the *accepted* "Creator"), is or would be worse than the most loquacious idiot—poor body! But if the great anguish issues out of something much higher behind it—though why it would in such a manner is hard to imagine—then it too *may* be better than it seems, possibly morally justifiable, though *how* must for me (not being an archbishop or even a curate) remain a sad puzzle, since, to my own moral sense—which is the only one I have—nothing *can* justify injustice. The tusk of an aged mammoth has,

I believe, been discovered somewhere in such a horrible, though now happily petrified, state of inflammation at the roots as must have meant constant, violent toothache; just think of *that* and of a mammoth's tusk—if *both* were not affected! Did the poor great beast deserve it more than the best, or even worst man of the same period would have done in some equivalent way—for *he* might have knocked out his tooth? Surely not, for what could all three have been other than products of inevitability?

'But, however, I am only an agnostic and agnosticism—hitherto the only balm in Gilead or elsewhere for a universe which needs it so badly—may perhaps, through the class of fact here dwelt upon, become just a thought balmier. "Sweet bodements! good!"—as far as they go at least, possibly, in this present scanty statement of them relating to one species only. They are, however, widely supported by all those other varied observations which I have made and hitherto had to keep to myself from a widespread conviction amongst publishers that nobody *could* be sufficiently interested in *such* a subject to buy—much less read—a book about them in all this bird-loving land!'

But here we have the first description of the duetting of the whooper swan in Iceland (from *The Realities of Bird Life*, 1927).

'It was happily while they were thus observable through the glasses that they broke twice, at intervals, into a clamorous duet of strained clanging cries, extremely loud and powerful, bursting out suddenly and simultaneously, as in a sort of frenzy, and continuing for two or three minutes—at least it seemed so. These outbursts were not, as before, ushered in by the melancholy wailing note, which is now absent *in toto*. In thus clamouring the birds stretched their necks straight out in front of them all along the water, as they had done on other occasions, but I now noticed that, instead of the head and neck being all in one straight line, the former was raised a little above the water and then bent sharply down again. This gave them a strange wild look with which the clangorous cries seemed in harmony. They first swam towards each other, then followed one another in line, and finally went side by side clamouring all the time in this way—a sight for sair een. That they felt intensely, whilst going through with it, seemed evident . . . Each time, after this concert, there was a moment or two of what seemed the awakening of sexual activities.'

Not surprisingly Selous was largely neglected or despised by the stuffy museum ornithologists of his day; yet ultimately his influence was great, for he it was who largely inspired later workers such as H. Eliot Howard, F. B. Kirkman, Julian Huxley, and Edward Armstrong. All these have an excellent and sometimes distinguished literary style and so the message of Selous came through to the scientific world mainly at secondhand. Of this group of four, only Julian Huxley ranked as a professional zoololgist.

Eliot Howard, a sound observer and thinker, who was the founder of the modern concept of territory in bird life, was a successful Worcestershire businessman who can have had little time for his observations apart from the dawn hours and weekends. Kirkman was also an amateur, a fine observer deeply sensitive to the psychological state of his subjects; while Edward Armstrong (after a journey round the world) wrote the standard textbook *Bird Display and Behaviour* while still curate of a Leeds slum parish.

Julian Huxley, who was greatly stimulated both by Selous and Howard, published in 1914 the first of a classic series of studies of the courtship displays of grebes and allied birds, considering these in relation to Darwin's theory of sexual selection. It is significant, and very intriguing, that for long he regarded this work simply as his recreation and relied upon his studies on comparative physiology as his real claim to scientific advancement. In his memoirs he reminds himself how during his first appointment as a Demonstrator at Balliol College he organized a reading party during which he stupidly waded his way through an enormous German work on the Protozoa while in his spare time doing something which he knew intuitively would be of much greater importance in the long run: namely scientific bird watching.

But one other professional scientist, F. H. A. Marshall, a lecturer in physiology at Cambridge who was in the 1920s already a world authority on the physiology of reproduction, produced in 1936 and 1942 two papers on sexual periodicity and the internal and external (perceptual) factors which govern it. These papers of Marshall's immediately began to shed light on the mechanisms whereby perception of the extraordinary stimulus patterns, provided, for instance, by the display antics of a male bird, could be influencing and entraining the sexual and reproductive behaviour of the female. Marshall's work immediately secured attention from the professional physiologists but few ornithologists realised at the time the implication it had for their subject—far greater than that of any other physiological work of the period. It was the wide range of Armstrong's book, penetrating as it does the physiological, psychological, and philosophical fields, which was perhaps the major stimulus in the early forties to the strictly ornithological fraternity. Eliot Howard (1929, 1935, 1940) and E. A. Armstrong (1942, 1947) were, I think, the only amateurs that took immediate notice of Marshall's work, and it was through them that it made its first impact on ornithologists in general. Even Howard's work (apart from his famous *Territory in Bird Life*, 1290) did not immediately make the impact one might have expected. This was perhaps due to his style of publication. His book *The British Warblers: A History with Problems of their Lives* appeared between 1907 and 1914 and in every sense was a pioneer *tour de force*: but its publication in a deluxe limited edition rendered it not too easy of access to the amateur even though it broke entirely new ground as a natural history study. Later works* which show the influence of Marshall, namely *An Introduction to Bird Behaviour* (1929), *The Nature of the Bird's World* (1935) and *A Waterhen's World* (1940), seem not to have had the influence which their deep understanding of avian nature warranted. And they again were in extremely deluxe format.

Finally, to conclude this chapter, I must mention that it was the pioneer work and enthusiasm of Julian Huxley and F. B. Kirkman which led to the foundation in 1936 of the 'Institute [now Association] for the Study of Animal Behaviour'.

* All by H. E. Howard.

REFERENCES

1. Gray, P. H., 'Spalding and his influence on developmental behaviour', *J. Hist. behav. Sci.*, 1967, **3**, 168–79.
2. Spalding, D. A., *Nature*, 1872, **6**, 485–6.
3. Spalding, D. A., *Macmillan's Magazine*, 1873, **27**, 282–93.
4. Hume, D., *A Treatise of Human Nature* (London: John Noon, 1783).
5. Gray, P. H., 'Verification of Spalding's method for controlling visual experience by hooding chicks in the shell', *Proc. Montana Acad. Sci.*, 1961, **21**, 120–3.
6. Spalding, op. cit. (1873).
7. Gray, op. cit. (1967), p. 171.
8. Spalding, D. A., *Nature*, 1875, **12**, 507–8.
9. Boring, E. G., *History of Experimental Psychology*, 2nd edn. (New York: Apleton-Century Crofts Inc., 1950).
10. Gray, P. H., 'The Morgan–Romanes controversy', *Proc. Montana Acad. Sci.*, 1963, **23**, 225–30.
11. For a fuller summary of Lloyd Morgan's contributions see Adler, H. E., *Ann. N.Y. Acad. Sci.*, 1973, **223**, 41–8.
12. See especially Griffin, D. R., *The Question of Animal Awareness* (New York: Rockefeller University Press, 1976).

4

Ethology in the United States of America 1880–1940

In the United States the years 1880–1940 constituted a period of rapid scientific advance. I have no space to trace the great developments in straight animal natural history although it certainly would be well worth doing. Of these, L. H. Morgan, *The American Beaver and his Works*[1] perhaps came nearer than any other to the modern ethological ideal. But there were four or five outstanding figures in zoology, giants they were indeed, who prepared the way for the coming of ethology and nearly got there first on their own. I put first Charles Otis Whitman, who was the commanding genius in the zoological field for about thirty years from the early 1880s. Whitman's first professional work was in embryology though he early showed a predilection for comparative phylogenetic studies of behaviour. He is said to have kept pigeons as a boy and 'to be fascinated by them, sitting watching them by the hour, intensely interested in their feeding, their young and everything they did'.[2] Whitman's classic studies of pigeon behaviour were not published until 1919, long after his death; and one might assume from this that he regarded such work as a hobby and not in the main line of his contributions to zoology. However, I think this is incorrect for he made his views known much earlier; especially by the lecture 'Animal Behaviour' given at Woods Hole.[3] In this he developed a series of four maxims, resulting from his studies of the leech *Clepsine* and the mud-puppy *Necturus* (and of course pigeons) designed to guide students concerned with the comparative behaviour of animals in their natural environment:

1. Instincts are evolved not improvised and their genealogy may be as complex and far-reaching as the history of their organic bases.
2. The first criterion of instinct is that it can be performed by the animal without learning by experience, instruction, or imitation. The first performance is therefore the crucial one.
3. The main guidance for getting at the phyletic history of animals must be comparative study.
4. Plasticity of instinct is not intelligence; but it is the open door through which the great educator, experience, comes in and works every wonder of intelligence.

He also, in a sentence which has been hailed as initiating the birth of modern ethology, said 'instincts and organs are to be studied from the common viewpoint of phyletic descent'. My impressions on reading this lecture are two-fold. First is the originality and modernity of his outlook. Second is the absence of reference to any European studies. The only non-United States workers mentioned are Lloyd Morgan and Karl Groos (*The Play of Animals*, 1894) and the entomologists Kirby and Spence. From the USA William James is relied upon; his *Textbook of Psychology* (1892) is a classic though only very general summary of the subject.

During this period the writings of Jacques Loeb and J. von Uexküll were being avidly studied and were exerting a great influence. Loeb (1859-1924) achieved wide fame as a zoologist as a result of his enunciation of the concepts of 'forced movements' or 'tropisms' as the essential basis for interpreting the facts of the behaviour of organisms. He was a Prussian who started in philosophy as a result of early fascination with the writings of Schopenhauer and Hartmann: the 'philosophers of the will'. In fact he resolved to become a philosopher in order to show that the will is *not* free! But he was so disillusioned by his philosophy professors at Berlin, whom he described as mere 'wordmongers', that he abandoned the subject and turned to biology. In this field he was an apostle of mechanistic conceptions—possibly because, as an ardent Francophile, he sought to harness his empirical researches to the philosophical concerns of the '*philosophes*'. His work was stimulating and valuable to the biology of its time in that his theories were clear, simple, and readily tested experimentally; and his influence extended greatly when he came to live in the USA. For the simpler movements of plants and of the simplest animals his explanations contained much that was sound and plausible. But when pressed further it was found, as indeed followers of D'Arcy Thompson's great work[4] discovered in a later generation, that the physics and chemistry of the time were as yet too simplistic to bear the weight which the biologists wished to place upon them. And in Loeb's case his theories, when applied to animals of any considerable degree of anatomical complexity, were found to be woefully inadequate. For it is now known[5] that the behaviour of even a sea-anenome is vastly more complex than anyone had previously supposed.

A particularly valuable corrective to the tropism theory of Loeb came from H. S. Jennings (1868–1947), renowned for his work on coelenterates and echinoderms and above all for his book *The Behaviour of the Lower Organisms* (1906). He studied the behaviour of protozoa such as *Paramoecium* and *Amoeba* (to mention only two) with far greater exactitude than had ever been done before. Some of his results with the former went far to support Loeb's conclusions; but he saw many of the deeper implications which Loeb missed, and in regard to *Amoeba* he made the oft-quoted remark, 'The writer is thoroughly convinced, after a long study of the behaviour of *Amoeba*, that if it were a large animal, so as to come within the everyday experience of human-beings, its behaviour would at once call forth the attribution to it of pleasure and pain, of hunger, desire and the like, on precisely the same basis as we attribute these things to a dog.' He said this as a simple statement of opinion and we must not read into it any devotion to a crude vitalism, for that he certainly did not, I am sure, intend. But he did probe deep into the problem of the brain and its relation to the overwhelming question of consciousness in ourselves, and in particular the genetical aspects of the uniqueness of human personal experience. To discuss this here would take us too far afield; but those interested will find a discussion of the matter in my *Animal Nature and Human Nature*.[6]

Another pioneer was Wallace Craig (1876–1954), a pupil of Whitman, whose studies of doves reared in isolation, of doves learning to drink, and above all his paper on *Appetites and Aversions as Constituents of Instincts* (1918) were of great theoretical importance and have been warmly and consistently acknowledged in modern ethological literature.

In a series of less than a dozen papers published during the years 1908–43 (most of them commendably brief), Craig put forward original ideas on four or five topics which were just becoming of central interest for ethology. First was the problem of appetitive behaviour. He regarded 'appetite' as a condition that showed itself externally as a state of agitation which continued for as long as a certain stimulus—he used the ugly phrase 'appeted stimulus'—is absent. He said, 'When the appeted stimulus is at length received, it stimulates a consummatory reaction, after which the appetitive behaviour ceases and is succeeded by a state of relative rest.' He also employed the concept of aversion in the opposite sense, as a state of agitation which continues as long as a certain stimulus (referred to as the 'disturbing stimulus') is present, but which wanes when that stimulus has ceased to act on the sense organs and is replaced by a state of relative rest. He points out that appetitive behaviour is thus, from one point of view, a reaction to the absence of something, and this is exactly what Lashley meant when he spoke of instinct being a reaction to a deficit. It may be convenient here to give one example, although of course many others may be found in the pages that follow, of an appetite for an instinctive or consummatory action pattern. A dove, exhibiting nest-building activity for the first time, continually picks up straws with a characteristic innate movement and shows a tendency to build them into some sort of nest. When an *experienced* bird first finds a straw, he seizes it immediately and toys with it, sometimes making movements resembling those by which he would build the straw into a nest. This *seems* to generate an appetite for building the straw in (although we cannot in this case rule out independent fluctuations in the drive as a cause of the observed behaviour change), and when this appetite is sufficiently aroused he flies to the nest, guided by associative memory, and performs the consummatory act completely. The young female continues toying with the straw an excessively long time, not carrying it at all, even though she may be very near the nest, but at length, when she does go to the nest with her straw, she makes well-ordered, apparently instinctive movements to build it in.

The same sort of thing is apparent in an *inexperienced* young male dove locating a nesting-site for the first time. At first the dove, standing on his perch, spontaneously assumes the nest-calling attitude—body thrown forward and head down, as if neck and breast were already touching the hollow of the nest—and while in this attitude the nest-call is sounded; but all the time he shows dissatisfaction, as if the perch were not a comfortable situation for this behaviour. He shifts about and performs the action, first in one place and then in another, until he finds a corner which more or less fits his body when in this posture. He is seldom satisfied with the first corner found, but tries one after another and then perhaps comes back to the first. If now a suitable nest-box, or ready-made nest, is put into the cage, the inexperienced bird does not recognise it as a nest, but sooner or later he tries it for nest-calling, and in such trial the nest evidently gives him a strong and satisfying stimulation—a stimulation which no other circumstance has supplied. In the nest his attitude becomes enhanced; he turns from side to side, moving the straws with beak, feet, breast, and wings as if, to quote Wallace Craig, 'rioting in the wealth of new luxurious stimuli'. He no longer wanders restlessly in search of new nesting situations, but remains satisfied with his present highly stimulating nest.

It seems fairly clear from the latter example that there is no innate visual recognition of the nest as something appropriate; the bird has to get into it and experience its characteristics with other senses besides vision before he, as it were, realises its possibilities. And there is, of course, a great deal of appetitive behaviour in which the locomotory or other activity is largely random, being merely restricted within certain rather ill-defined limits. Obviously the male dove does not search for a nest site outside the territory which it is inhabiting at that moment, probably it does not look for sites on the ground; but presumably if it wanders sufficiently persistently through that restricted region it will find any appropriate stimulus that may be there.

As another example, Craig pointed to the issue of expectancy. His point is that in order for learning to occur, the reinforcement must in some sense confirm an expectancy. Now, of course, we must not for a moment assume that on its first performance of an appetitive action the animal necessarily 'knows' what its behaviour should lead to. It is abundantly clear that, in many cases at least, it cannot possibly do so. But there is also good evidence that on first performing an innate consummatory act, organisms will show some evidence of surprise—a form of the '*ah-ha erlebnis*' of Bühler. The behaviour is such as to suggest that the animal is expecting 'something' *but does not know what*, having perhaps an extremely generalized or elementary innate releasive mechanism. By trial and error it acquires, perhaps extremely slowly, perhaps very imperfectly, an insight into, a perception of, temporal relations; a—to quote Tolman's vivid but awkward phrase—'what-leads-to-what' expectancy. And this *understanding* is the essential basis of reinforcement in a trial and error learning situation.

In a paper published in 1914 on the behaviour of male doves reared in isolation Craig stressed the value of practice as providing a fine adjustment of an instinctively coded technique. He says, 'When a male dove performs an instinctive act for the first time, it generally shows some surprise, hesitation, bewilderment or even fear; and the first performance is in a mechanical, reflex style, whereas the same act after much experience is performed with ease, skill and intelligent adaptation.' Some further evidence along these lines will be found in Volume III (pp. 156–59) of C. O. Whitman's great work.[7]

Craig also made acute observations on young doves learning to drink. In this case the innate drinking activity consists of bending the head low and swallowing. Originally the act of swallowing is released only by the stimulus of water on the inside of the mouth, and the dove shows no innate tendency to produce the drinking response at the sight or sound of water, nor to the presence of water on the distal parts of the body, such as the tail or wings—although there may occasionally be a slight response as a result of the contact of water with the feet. The first drink probably results from an accidental pecking of some conspicuous or shining object in or on water, or possibly just by pecking at the sparkling surface. Pigeons are particularly ready to peck at glistening objects, and anything which catches their attention may bring about this first drink. The drinking movements are thus innate, but the bird has no concept of water as being the stuff to drink and takes some considerable time to learn. Thus one dove which was studied showed no evidence, on the second and third occasion of drinking, of having remembered the first experience, but from the fourth time onward it showed clear evidence of memory. It quickly learned to associate the action of drinking water with all sorts of stimuli, such as the shape and appearance of the dish, the person who brought the dish, and the sound of water being poured out, etc., but it took much longer for it to recognise water as such, and even a thirsty dove would make no attempt to drink if the dish in which the water was presented was unfamiliar. During this period the doves would not infrequently make drinking movements as soon as they saw the approach of the dish but before it had reached them. Sometimes they would stand in the dish and put the bill down outside it, appearing to be disappointed that the drink was unsuccessful.

Wallace Craig was far in advance of his time in making a highly effective study of bird-song before the modern methods of recording and analysis were available—arguing that true vocal imitation in bird-song must be regarded as a late development from inherited song patterns, and is characteristic of the most highly evolved amongst the true song-birds. He cites, as other students of bird-song have done, the evidence for deliberate aesthetic improvement of song (as witness the repeated 'practice' of song phrases by particularly 'gifted' individuals) as being by no means negligible. Craig was the first to propose this as a result of a long and detailed study of the Tyrranid flycatcher *Contopus virens* (the eastern wood pewee). There is now much more evidence for the 'aesthetic view' than there was when Craig wrote.

This matter was considered by Lorenz (in correspondence with Craig[8]) in connexion with the evolution of tonal purity in bird voices. Lorenz had made the point that the purity of colour of some visual social releasers (as in the duck's speculum) could be of selective value since they have to be seen against a complex inanimate or non-animal background containing every shade of colour. Song, he argues, encounters virtually no non-biological competition, since there are practically no sounds of inanimate origin which are of such frequency or form as to compete[9].

But hardly second to Whitman and certainly as a savant of encyclopaedic erudition the greatest of all, was William Morton Wheeler (1865–1937). Wheeler can claim to be the first in the English-speaking world who used the term 'ethology' in its present-day meaning (a meaning he almost certainly obtained from the French—from Fabre and probably also Giard). Between 1902 and 1905 he published several papers saying that zoologists were much in need of a satisfactory term for animal behaviour. Then he went on, 'the only term hitherto suggested which will adequately express the study of animals with a view to elucidating their true character and expressing in their physical and psychical behaviour towards their living and inorganic environment is ethology.'[10] As we have seen, Isidore Geoffroy-Saint-Hilaire used the word in the sense of scientific natural history and it was accepted by the annual *Zoological Record*, published by the Zoological Society of London, in the 1901 volume as a heading for studies of 'habits and instincts'; later the Zoological Record became confused, first including ethology under ecology and then *vice versa* with ecology as a sub-heading of ethology, until it finally dropped 'ethology' altogether!

Wheeler continued using the term 'ethology' and produced in 1917 a brilliant essay on the subject of instinct which was re-published in *Essays of Philosophical Biology* (Harvard University Press, 1939). But for some curious reason, his use of the term 'ethology' did not stick in the United States and he is now chiefly remembered as the great pioneer in the study of insect societies and as the world authority on ants. I only met him once, to my great regret, but this was enough to glimpse his immense mental

Figure 2 William Morton Wheeler. Figure by kind permission
of the Harvard University Press.

stature. He was a polyglot, reading classical languages with ease,
equally at home with French, German, and Italian. He was
widely read in philosophy, psychology, and sociology, and a
great student of the Bible. His industry was overwhelming. He
belittled his immense taxonomic work on ants by saying that he
described his ants as a useful hobby in the same sense that his
wife did her knitting. With Wheeler, physiologist Lawrence J.
Henderson, philosopher Alfred North Whitehead, and H. L.
Taylor formed a little philosophical coterie in Harvard whose
conversation must have been exciting beyond measure. Indeed,
one of his colleagues said of Wheeler that there was no man

living more suited to carry on a conversation with Aristotle.

Wheeler's critical and polemical writing could be both pungent and extremely amusing. Thus he attacked the views of the famous Jesuit student of ants, Erich Wasmann, as an example of the misunderstandings and deficiencies of the then current ideas of insect behaviour held by some of the specialists on ants. Wasmann had claimed that the relationships between ants and their myrmecophiles could not be explained by natural selection but that special 'symphilic instincts' had arisen as modifications of the ants' original brood-rearing instincts. He also tended to misuse the word 'mimicry' as applied to ant guests, apparently thinking that the similarity of the ant models and their mimics could only have been produced by special creation. Wheeler replied, 'If three of my maiden aunts are fond of pets and prefer cats, parrots, and monkeys respectively I am not greatly enlightened when the family physician takes me aside and informs me sententiously that my Aunt Eliza undoubtedly has an aelurophilous, my Aunt Mary a psittacophilous, and my Aunt Jane a pithecophilous instinct, and that the possession of these instincts satisfactorily explains their behaviour.'

A great achievement of Wheeler in relation to animal behaviour was his discovery of the phenomenon of trophallaxis, i.e. secretions provided by some individuals and castes in the ant societies which attract and reward the attention of other individuals and castes; thus binding the colony into a whole. This discovery, which was the forerunner of the present work on pheromones in insects, brought clarity and understanding into the study of insect societies; a field which had previously been confused and confounded by the postulation of numerous mysterious *ad hoc* instincts and tendencies.

One of Wheeler's many famous pupils was A. C. Kinsey. When the latter switched from entomology to sexology Wheeler characteristically summed up a part of his work as follows:

'Evidently a very considerable proportion of the population is over-sexed, under-sexed, intersexed or no-sexed, and, therefore, not well suited to family life of the old-fashioned, rural, or garden variety. It is of course very easy to tell these people to go to hell, but many of them are so devilishly attractive and, apart from their sexual behaviour, so very efficient socially, that they are constantly being married by those who are blessed with normal sexual proclivities and ideals.'

And if these giants were not enough there was yet another to come, namely Karl Spencer Lashley. Early in his career Lashley had worked with J. B. Watson on the nesting behaviour of noddy and sooty terns, but, reacting against Watson's behaviourism, he soon broke away and became, with his doctrines of 'mass action' and 'equipotentiality', one of the great brain physiologists of his time.

But the great importance of Lashley to ethology was not primarily his powerful analysis of cortical function and organization of the brain. It was rather his gifts as an observer and interpreter of the behaviour of the whole animal, especially in its social relationship—in short his powers as a naturalist. He had in fact been an enthusiastic naturalist and pet-keeper as a boy and this attitude had animated his work on the terns just mentioned. He returned to the behaviour field as a successor to R. M. Yerkes in 1941 when he took over the Primate (Chimpanzee) Research Station at Orange Park, Florida.

Yerkes (1876–1956) did not possess an ethological cast of mind in any strict sense, though his work in the long term greatly furthered the growth of the subject. But he was a pioneer comparative psychologist: perhaps the principal developer of the subject in the USA. He had studied 'intelligence' in a great variety of animals during his Harvard period—from jellyfish and crabs through to pigs, primates, and man (a study which, it is only fair to say, showed up the deficiencies—indeed the dangers—of the use of this word unless defined with the utmost exactness). On being appointed to a chair at Yale in 1924 he had the opportunity to start work on the primates in a big way and founded the Orange Park field station and laboratories as a centre for the study of the neural and physiological bases for the behaviour of primates. His work there paved the way for Lashley in an admir-

Figure 3 Karl Spencer Lashley. Figure by kind permission of
the National Academy of Sciencies

able manner, providing the foundations on which the latter
could build.

So Lashley, when he was established at Orange Park, became,
in addition to being a neurophysiologist of towering fame, one of
the leading primatologists of the world. Yet his ethological
achievement stemmed from the fact that in 1938 he wrote a
paper on the experimental analysis of instinctive behaviour[11]
which, independently of Lorenz, but almost exactly at the same
time, expressed almost every point of importance which came to
characterize the ethological view of instinct.

Lashley realised that the aspect of instinct which would be most rewarding of close study was not specifically the drive itself, but rather the internal system of co-ordination of special behaviour patterns on the one hand and the special receptive sensory mechanisms on the other. In fact, he concentrated his attention on the whole specific sensori-motor organization of the behaviour patterns, considering the complex and stereotyped action system to be more fundamental to the subject than any question of drive. He suggested that a study of these mechanisms themselves might throw light on the problems of internal drive and motivation. Earlier, Woodworth in his system of *Dynamic Psychology* (1918) had attempted a similar approach, and had pointed out that habit mechanisms, at any rate in human beings, may become drives; implying that, since in his view and that of many earlier writers, habit and instinct had much in common, the co-ordinating mechanism of the behaviour pattern itself might be generating the drive. This view was strongly criticized at the time, but, at least as far as habit is concerned, Woodworth did produce some substantial arguments. These were taken up by Lashley who suggested that *all* cases of motivation might well turn out to be of this nature. That is to say that physiologically, all drives are no more than expressions of the activity of *specific* mechanisms, and that a general drive is really nothing more nor less than the partial excitation of a very specific sensori-motor mechanism irradiating to affect other systems of reaction.

Why then did not ethology come into its full flowering in the USA? In my view it was, as I shall proceed to argue, delayed by the dominance of the already established 'behaviourism'. This problem was highlighted for me personally by a visit to Harvard as a lecturer in 1951. I was then giving a course of lectures covering modern developments in animal behaviour studies and I naturally had a good deal to say about Whitman, Wheeler, and Wallace Craig. After about my second lecture, Professor Boring, doyen of American psychologists, said to me, 'Did you know that Wallace Craig was in the audience?' I was astounded as I had supposed him dead!

I then made enquiries and found that there seemed to be only two people in a large audience who knew who he was and what he had done and only one of them knew that he had been living in Cambridge, Mass., for years! However, better late than never, I made his acquaintance and had some pleasant discussions with him. It was characteristic of his retiring nature that he did not make himself known to me after one of my lectures.

It was a lucky time to be lecturing in the USA because I already possessed Niko Tinbergen's *Study of Instinct* (which had not yet appeared in the United States) not to mention the advantage of my close friendship with both Niko and Konrad. So practically everything I was saying was new to my audience! Of course, Niko's book soon became widely read in America and it was, I am sure, the main factor in finally getting ethology airborne in the USA.

Another very interesting part of the visit was getting to know both Lashley and Skinner. Skinner clearly had little use for ethology and what struck me (as a result of watching his pigeons at work in their Skinner boxes) was the great variety of displacement activity, appetitive behaviour, etc., which was proceeding all the time and, of course, going unobserved. This was obviously regarded by Skinner as of no interest whatsoever and its investigation a simple waste of time. When I told Skinner that we were going down to Orange Park, Florida to visit Lashley he said acidly, 'Why bother to see Lashley? You won't learn anything from him!' When we got to Orange Park we soon realised that Lashley regarded the appointment of Skinner to the major chair of Psychology at Harvard as one of the greatest disasters to have befallen that University in recent times! In fact Lashley was also a Professor in Harvard—although he resided in Orange Park in his *alter ego* as Director of the Research Station there. His professorship however necessitated his giving a few lectures annually at Harvard and this he managed to do by some extraordinary arrangement which involved delivering them all in about the space of a fortnight so that he could get away to Orange Park again as soon as possible—the reason for his distaste of the Harvard atmosphere being obvious!

Skinner's views on ethology later mellowed somewhat and

when he spent a term in Cambridge, England, about ten or twelve years ago his readiness to break off his writing (which was the main objective of his sabbatical leave) and travel widely to address almost any small group of students when invited, created a very favourable impression.

Lashley was an extraordinarily attractive character; a thin, charming, hyperactive man with a delightful sense of humour and great mental agility. He was also an accomplished musician, particularly as a string player. His thinking was so quick that when lecturing he poured out an almost overwhelming torrent of words which must have been incomprehensible to the elementary student. His was a mind completely devoted to the discovery of truth even though this meant pulling to pieces and destroying a beautiful theory of his own. He would come up with some exciting results or some improvement of technique in the study of animal learning or of brain function, would publish this and then immediately think of a new technique which would give a fresh angle or more accurate results. He would employ this and when, as not infrequently happened, he showed his early theory to be wrong— instead of being crestfallen, he would be hugely delighted and would exult in publicly knocking down his own theoretical structure. This trait was so marked that I really believe it resulted in his not having the research following in the United States that his great eminence and ability might have led one to expect. It seems that his mental agility and self-criticism confused and alienated all except the most brilliant students; for, they thought, if the great Lashley can be as wrong as this, what chance is there in this field for poor 'bods' like ourselves? Be this as it may, it offers a plausible reason for his failure to achieve the full conceptual scheme of animal behaviour which we now regard as the central achievement of Konrad Lorenz. The more one studies the American situation at that time the more extraordinary it seems that the American group did not become the modern founders of ethology. They came so near it and were well in advance of workers anywhere else in the world.

Perhaps some explanation is to be found in the rise of behaviourism. From 1898 to 1911 Thorndike, motivated, it seems, by hearing Lloyd Morgan lecture in Boston in 1896, elaborated his study based on observations on cats in puzzle boxes. This led to a theory of animal behaviour which was quickly taken up by Watson—a system which was fundamentally associationist or 'mechanist' in outlook and prided itself upon being purely objective—with the implication that it was of a physiological rather than a psychological nature. Perhaps we should have heard less about Watson's behaviourism had it not been that in the few years from its publication the work of Pavlov and Bekhterev began to be known outside Russia. And so, for the first time, there seemed to be a physiological system which could be related in detail to the superficially physiological ideas behind behaviouristic psychology. Behaviourism was in some ways a laudible attempt to be objective and to purge behavioural study of the uncritical anecdotal writings previously felt inimical to its progress; but 'behaviourism' as a general theory of animal behaviour had fatal deficiencies. Nevertheless the tremendous success and obviously immense importance of Pavlovian conditioning theory in the form in which it struck the United States through Watson (but from which his old colleague Lashley vigorously dissented) may go some way to explain the long period of adolescence of the indigenous American ethology.

REFERENCES

1. Morgan, L. H., *The American Beaver and His Works* (Philadelphia, 1868).
2. Lilley, F. R., *J. Morphology*, 1911, **22**, xv–lxviii.
3. 16th Woods Hole Biological Lecture for 1898.
4. Thompson, D'A., *On Growth and Form*, 2nd edn. (Cambridge University Press, 1941).
5. Pantin, C. F. A., *The Relations Between the Sciences* (Cambridge University Press, 1968).
6. Thorpe, W. H., *Animal Nature and Human Nature* (London: Methuen; New York: Doubleday-Anchor, 1974), pp. 326–9.
7. Whitman, C. O., 'The behaviour of pigeons', *Posthumous Works of C. O. Whitman* (1919), Vol. **3**, pp. 156–9.
8. Craig, W., 'The Song of the Wood Pewee' (*Myochanes virens*), *New York State Mus. Bull.*, **334**, pp. 6–186 (see p. 161).

9. For a modern summary of the massive developments in the field of vocal communication in birds, see Hinde, R. A. (Editor), *Bird Vocalizations: their relation to current problems in biology and psychology* (essays presented to W. H. Thorpe) (Cambridge: CUP, 1969) and *Non-verbal Communication* (Cambridge: CUP, 1972) especially Chapter 6 by Thorpe, W. H.

10. Wheeler, W. M., ' "Natural history", "oecology" or "ethology" ', *Science n.s.*, 1902, **15**, 971–6.

11. Lashley, K. S., 'The experimental analysis of instinctive behaviour', *Psychol. Rev.*, 1938, **45**, 445–71.

5

The establishment of ethology in continental Europe (1910–50)

It fell to workers in Austria, Germany, and Holland to effect the final establishment of ethology as we now know it. Apart from Alfred Giard, the first person deliberately to use the term 'ethology' in its modern connotation in this period was Oscar Heinroth. This was in a major paper (1911) to which most of the modern workers in Europe attribute their first inspirations. He also wrote a large number of small papers over many years; and together with his wife produced a major book on the birds of middle Europe (1924–33) which contains a great deal of original observation of an ethological nature. Heinroth does not quote any previous worker for his use of the term 'ethology' but it seems evident that he owed it primarily to Giard who, as we have seen, was using it frequently till towards the end of his life in 1908. It is also important to stress that Heinroth is often given the credit of being the first to use the term *Prägung* (imprinting). However he never seems to have specifically acknowledged the influence of Douglas Spalding; though surely he must have been aware of it.

What Heinroth did achieve for ethology was to make abundantly clear to ornithologists and other students of vertebrate behaviour that behaviour patterns (as in the ducks) can be reliably used to provide evidence for the systematic relationships between species; and as a basis for theorizing about the detailed course of evolution of such characters. This had been obvious to entomologists for a long time, and had been incorporated in systems of classification. But the hard cuticle of insects ordinarily provides such a wealth of 'characters' suitable for taxonomy; visible, if not to the naked eye, at least under a hand-lens; that it was otiose to employ behavioural characters *per se* in classification.

It is hardly necessary to say more about Heinroth here; it will suffice to note that Konrad Lorenz claimed Heinroth as the source of his inspiration and in one place he strangely defined ethology as 'the subject which Heinroth invented'. Tinbergen is equally clear about his debt to Heinroth. We can therefore proceed further and pause to mention briefly some who were Lorenz's seniors and who, although they did not use the term 'ethology', certainly had a seminal influence on its early development. I refer particularly to Jakob von Uexküll (1864–1944) and of course Karl von Frisch.

Von Uexküll was a remarkable figure, a highly original individualist whose work on animal nature, first summarized in his book *Umwelt und Innenwelt der Tiere* (1909), had a subtle influence on the thinking of biologists of his day. He was a 'Baltic Baron' of great mental stature, of independent means and of an even more independent spirit. After the first World War his independent means had dwindled to a large extent, but his spirit remained unbroken through this and all subsequent crises; he could not even be silenced when attacked in the German press by Goebbels in person.

Looked at from the point of view of the contemporary scientific establishment he must have seemed to many a wild nonconformist. He had studied zoology in Dorpat for four years. At first greatly attracted by Darwinian teachers, he gradually began to feel that they were overstating their case, and turned his attention to physiology. At the same time he started taking an interest in the philosophy of Kant, and developed a form of 'vitalism' which was later much decried. He left Dorpat after taking the degree of 'Candidate of Zoology'. Although this corresponded roughly to the German Ph.D. the terminological difference caused eventually great difficulties vis-à-vis the academic bureaucrats in Germany. All went well as long as von Uexküll was of independent means. He lived a happy and active

Figure 4 Jakob von Uexküll. Photo by Olga Linkelmann. Taken on his seventieth birthday, 8th September 1934. Kindly supplied by Dr Hans Lissmann.

life working on the physiology of nerves, muscle and sense organs in Heidelberg during the summer and in Naples during the winter. He enjoyed close friendships with many notable scientists, artists, and politicians of the Germany and Italy of his day: Robert Bunsen, Rainer Maria Rilke, Houston Stewart Chamberlain, and many others. His work at the Stazione Zoologica in Naples opened his eyes to the wealth of marine animals, and he soon established himself as one of the early founders of invertebrate physiology. He was a keen observer of both animals and man, and had a graphic way of putting his ideas into words. Thus having studied movements and reflexes of sea-urchins in some detail, he proclaimed: 'When a dog runs, the dog moves its legs—when a sea-urchin runs, the spines move the sea-urchin. The sea-urchin is a republic of reflexes.' While clever technical methods fascinated him—and he even went to Paris to learn from Marey the technique of cinematography—he also had a certain disdain for mere 'instrument physiologists'. He liked to tease some of his scientific friends by defining a 'scientific apparatus' as a source of error.

He laid great stress on simple, intelligent observation. For instance, physiologists of his time believed that there could be no reflex response without absorption of 'stimulus energy' through sense organs. Von Uexküll pointed out that many animals responded to a shadow, i.e. a non-stimulus or the withdrawal of light energy. His notions about the eye being more than a camera recall modern concepts of 'visual information processing', and if what he depicts as a 'function circle' were to be drawn as a block diagram we would instantly recognise the 'closed loop' of our present technological jargon.

Eventually he tired of pure nerve and muscle physiology for, as he said himself, to explore 'the harmonious co-operation of the organs within the animal body, seemed to me a more worthwhile task.' Thus he gradually shifted his interest to 'whole animal' biology, to the study of behaviour as an attempt to understand the subjective world (*Umwelt*) of each creature.

In his early days von Uexküll had felt that one important difficulty which had to be overcome was the generally accepted anthropocentric way of looking at animals. Thus people talked not only of a 'bloodthirsty polecat' but even of the 'spiritual life of infusoria'. Darwin himself had described the 'despair' of an ant at the destruction of its home. This was not a suitable way of 'solving' problems of sensory physiology. Therefore, together with Bethe and Beer (two well-known German physiologists), von Uexküll published in 1899 *A proposal for an objective nomenclature in the physiology of the nervous system,* substituting 'photoreception' for 'seeing', etc. This, they felt, would exclude at the outset all unwarranted assumptions about sensory experiences in other creatures. This proposal had an unforeseen and unexpected success which von Uexküll lived to regret: in the United States it triggered off a 'behaviourism' with extreme mechanistic interpretations (Watson), and Pavlov refers to the 'proposal' in his famous writings on 'conditioned reflexes'.

After the turbulence of the first World War had subsided,

(a)

(b)

Figure 5 The environment (a) and the umwelt (b) of the honey bee. After J. von Uexküll, kindly drawn by Priscilla Barrett.

von Uexküll, with the help of his physiologist friends, was established in an honorary Professorship of Biology with a very small department as part of the medical faculty of the University of Hamburg. By his charm and strength of personality, and with his great and varied zoological experience, he turned this tiny laboratory into an extraordinarily stimulating place of work. For the first time in his life he was faced with the task of teaching. His lectures were unconventional and attracted a motley audience of natural scientists, medical students, psychologists, and philosophers. His seminars were frank and open discussions, with the participants thinking aloud, and von Uexküll often settling a woolly argument with a pithy remark, a mixture of wisdom and naivety. But he was best in a man-to-man chat, when it soon became clear how much trouble he took over each of his research students and their problems. Von Uexküll's work had covered an enormous range on which he could now draw. Amongst other topics he had worked on the reflex physiology of echinoderms, cephalopods, and worms; on the nature of muscular contraction in leeches, dragonflies, bivalves, and brittle starfish; on chemical senses in aquatic animals. To this were added, in his laboratory in Hamburg, olfaction and territorial behaviour in dogs; behaviour of birds of prey and diving birds; sensory physiology of snakes, moles, and fish and many more.

In this happy and relaxed milieu quite a number of research students from the biological faculty found refuge—for the topics offered to prospective Ph.D. students in the Department of Zoology were not to everyone's taste; they consisted frequently in the task of having to count for three years the planktonic organisms which a number of professors had collected in countless bottles on criss-cross courses over the oceans of the world!

One of these 'refugees' was Hans Lissmann to whom I am greatly indebted for the reminiscences upon which this account of the Hamburg Biological Laboratory is based. Hans was from his early youth a 'tropical fish fancier'. He found in von Uexküll a sympathetic supporter of his project to base his doctoral thesis on research into fish behaviour. His great paper on the Siamese Fighting Fish (*Betta splendens*) *Die Umwelt des Kampffisches* (1932) was produced under von Uexküll's direction and has become one of the classic texts of ethology.

This drain of research students away from the Department of Zoology, together with the fact that von Uexküll was better known than the holders of posts in that department, led to jealousy and friction. The official disapproval was made known to the students, with the result that few of them dared to present themselves for examination at the Natural Sciences Faculty in Hamburg, but had to go to other universities to be examined. Von Uexküll himself remained aloof from all these squabbles. His only comment was: 'Amongst good scientists there is no competition, only co-operation. They are only trying to reveal the truth.' In that sense he was himself, as he had said of Bunsen, a 'giver', for the more one looks at the papers he wrote and the work he had obviously inspired, the more one becomes impressed by his great and beneficent influence on our subject. When open attacks in the Nazi press were added to inter-faculty difficulties, von Uexküll's laboratory went into decline; but by that time he had gained so much general respect that despite his outspokenness on all matters he came to no harm, and died peacefully on his beloved island of Capri in 1944.

Strange to relate it is not possible to describe adequately Karl von Frisch's scientific work without in the first place saying something about his family home. Before Karl was born his parents had made a habit of spending their summer holidays in the Salzkammergut region of Austria. One year they rented rooms in the water mill at Brunnwinkl on Lake Wolfgang. They fell in love with this spot, whereupon the owner of the mill, being almost bankrupt, asked them if they would like to buy it. This was an almost incredible piece of luck; not only the mill but a good deal of land on the lake shore nearby was purchased immediately. They turned the mill into a beautiful summer residence and converted another house into two summer villas; there were half-a-dozen other houses nearby which together made up the hamlet of Brunnwinkl. In due course the old mill which was the centre of it all became the permanent summer residence of the von Frisch family and the other houses were eventually occupied

Figure 6 Karl von Frisch. Photograph by W. Ernst Böhm. By kind permission of Pergamon Press. Frontispiece to *A Biologist Remembers*.

by three of Karl's maternal uncles. One or two other houses were taken over by distinguished scientists or literary men and one was occupied, and still is, by a small farmer. This little 'colony' is altogether charming and, as Karl von Frisch said, 'One has complete freedom—one can join in the relaxed family atmosphere or live as a complete hermit for days.' Karl's mother Marie (formerly Marie Exner) presided over the group and a high proportion of the children of the clan became good swimmers and climbers and ardent naturalists. And Karl's own development as a biologist obviously owed a good deal to this wonderful childhood environment. Even before the Brunnwinkl days he had a little zoo in his room in Vienna and when I visited the family at Brunnwinkl (now nearly thirty years ago) an exquisite little 'von Frisch Museum' of local natural history was a delight to the zoologist as well as to the amateur naturalist—and I believe is still so today.

Soon after graduation Karl became interested in fish biology and in particular in the sudden colour changes which fish, such as minnows, can show. He found by simple experiments that this reaction to light was not through the eyes but through a local effect of light on some pigment spots on the forehead of the fish just underneath a small translucent patch of skin. Underneath this there is an extension of the brain known as the pineal organ which appears to serve as a very primitive eye. This early discovery by Karl von Frisch has since provided several zoologists with a lifetime of work on the function of the pineal body. To mix one's metaphors, it was an extraordinary bull's eye as the first research of the young zoologist.

Karl did not follow up this particular topic himself, but it served to distract his attention to the vision of lower animals and especially the question of their ability to perceive colour. As a very young man Karl had realised that if any group of animals showed striking colour patterns it would be highly unlikely that they themselves lacked colour vision. Just at this time a distinguished Director of the Munich Eye Clinic, Karl von Hess, published experiments which led him to the conclusion that fish and, in fact, all invertebrate animals also, were completely colourblind. By this time Karl had found that fish could adapt their colour changes to that of their background and so von Hess's results seemed to him incredible. As soon as his experimental results were published he inevitably found himself engaged in an open war with von Hess: a conflict which continued over many years as Karl extended his work on colour vision to bees and many other animals. It was really a David and Goliath affair and in the end David won. But the whole acrimonious feud was a great trial and von Hess's response to Karl's work was disgraceful. Hess was not prepared even to consider von Frisch's experimental evidence, which in fact was conclusive; instead he tried to smother him with the great weight of his scientific authority. Karl is and always has been quiet, gentle, and serene. But he was furious that Hess should attempt to discredit his work and twist his statements in a misleading fashion and he wrote some raging rejoinders which were greatly disapproved of by some of Karl's seniors in zoology. In particular his former Professor and mentor, Richard von Hertwig, felt that it was improper to use immoderate language towards a man of von Hess's age and eminence. However, once Karl had proved himself indubitably right his rage abated and he soon ceased to harbour any rancour towards his erstwhile opponent. It was an unpleasant interlude and one which was quite foreign to the nature which Karl von Frisch has shown throughout his life. But in due course he came to feel that this violent controversy was not altogether bad and one wonders whether his life would have taken as happy and successful a turn without it; for it attracted the notice of his fellow scientists in a way which little else would have done.

Karl von Frisch's career as a scientist has been marked by a stately progression from one university chair to another, in increasing order of renown and prestige, culminating in the University of Munich. All the time Brunnwinkl remained his second home and it was nearly always possible to spend the summer vacations there carrying out his field research; at times with the help of members of his family and often latterly with the help of his visiting research students.

At Brunnwinkl, Karl had had a few beehives since his early twenties. The area is in fact not very suitable for beekeeping and good honey crops were a rarity; but in 1912 he started to do serious experiments with bees—again because many people still believed insects to be colourblind while he had the very firm hunch that of all insects, honey bees, whose whole life is bound up with foraging at flowers, must certainly have colour vision. The proof that bees did in fact possess a colour sense and his studies and investigations into the nature and extent of this vision was the first of his world famous series of investigations on *Apis mellifica*.

Karl's results on the dance language of the honey bee are so well known and have been described in so many popular works that it is hardly necessary to go into a full description of it here. Those who wish to refresh their memory can recall the essentials of the discovery by glancing at Figure 7. Karl first observed the honey bee dances in 1919 when he had a few bees feeding at a dish of weak sugar solution. These he first marked with red paint and then stopped from feeding for a while. As soon as all was quiet he filled the dish up again and watched a scout that had drunk from it after her return to the hive. He says, 'I could scarcely believe my

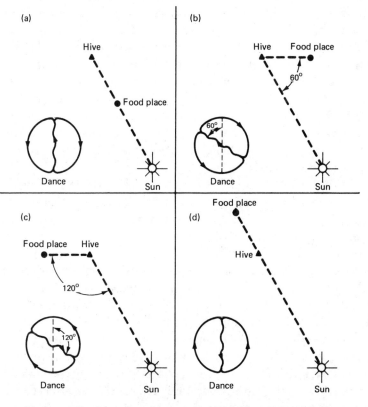

Figure 7 The dance language of the honey bee. Four examples of indication of direction. The sun is to the south-east of the hive. The diagram in each lower left corner shows schematically the direction of the waggle dance for a given position of the feeding place. From W. H. Thorpe, *Bulletin of Animal Behaviour*, no. 5, p. 31, 1947.

eyes. She performed a round dance on the honeycomb which greatly excited the marked foragers around her and caused them to fly back to the feeding place. This, I believe, was the most far-reaching observation of my life.' And that observation led to a whole series of papers from Karl and his associates (and ultimately many others too) up to the present day.

It is remarkable that one can find few scientists who have proceeded more steadily through a lifetime of research, with each paper showing new and seminal ideas coupled with simple but most elegant experiments—yet von Frisch is one of those who, if for a while his work did not progress satisfactorily, would feel himself a failure. In fact he would become depressed by the thought that each new investigation would be the last time that he had any ideas—a feeling which, it seems, he never completely overcame. Similarly, when he started his academic career he was afraid he would never be able to think up interesting enough subjects for students who might ask to write their theses under him. I cannot think of a living biologist who has had less reason to entertain such dreads!

Of course all stages in this epoch-making work were bound to be open to question, so revolutionary were the implications for our ideas as to the nature of the lower animals. So there were plenty of critics ready to do battle. But he never again lost his temper. He recalls vividly how one day when he was discussing his astonishing revelation that bees were sensitive to the polarization of light, he heard the deep bass of his uncle Sigmund Exner's voice remark in his driest manner, 'The explanation of most such extraordinary facts is simply that they are not true.'

To the ethologist (incidentally a term which Karl von Frisch seems never to have used) the most astonishing features of the dance communication of the honey bees (features not known for certain in any other invertebrate) are (a) that there are associational ties between signals of dance language and features in the outer world; and (b) that the dance language can refer to things in both time and space, i.e., what was found at a particular feeding source an hour ago or the day before, or even perhaps weeks before, proved the readiness with which the messages can be coined, for example a new rich source of food in a direction not previously investigated. These are matters of outstanding theoretical interest. In recent years, in fact almost up to the present moment, there have been disbelievers who thought they had shown that the dance of the bees were not really communicative and that it could all be explained by conditioning to particular odours in a particular environment. To go into this here would require far more space and more technical jargon than would be acceptable—suffice it to say that recent criticism by some workers in America, particularly that of Dr A. M. Wenner and his associates, have led to a very careful re-assessment and repetition of the key experiments—particularly those involving the powers of integration which are required if the dances are to carry their meaning without ambiguity. It is very pleasant to be able now to assert without fear of contradiction that while von Frisch may have at times underestimated the importance of the search for odours when finding a food source, his main results have been overwhelmingly confirmed, particularly by the work of J. L. Gould who, by most ingenious experiments, has confirmed Karl's conclusions up to the hilt.[1] Gould concludes his re-confirmation of von Frisch's results with the following words:

'Some of the resistance to the idea that honey bees possess a symbolic language seems to have arisen from a conviction that "lower" animals, and insects in particular, are too small and phylogenetically remote to be capable of "complex" behaviour. There is perhaps a feeling of incongruity in that the honey bee language is symbolic and abstract, and, in terms of information capacity at least, second only to human language. Despite expectations however, animals continue to be more complex than had been thought, or their experimenters may have been prepared to discover. Especially in ethology, it is difficult to avoid the unprofitable extremes of blinding scepticism and crippling romanticism.'

There are a number of other lines of research of great importance with which Karl von Frisch's name will be indissolubly associated, but his work on bees stands above them all for its brilliance, its economy, and its physiological and ethological significance, constituting a chain of observations and experiments begun in 1912 and continued until the present day.

We come now to another Austrian, also a Viennese, who is the key figure in the establishment of ethology in continental Europe during the period we are now considering. This is Konrad Zacharia Lorenz. Konrad Lorenz was born in 1903, the son of a distinguished orthopaedic surgeon in Vienna. The family home was, and indeed is, at Altenberg on the south bank of the Danube near the village of Greifenstein attractively situated where the hills of the Wienerwald come down to the Danube flood plain. The core of the homestead is an eighteenth-century farmhouse building which was greatly added to, with good taste for those times, by Konrad's father. From his earliest youth Konrad had a passion for natural history and the wild reaches of the Danube with its subsidiary streams, pools, rapids, and thickets was a marvellous place for a naturalist to grow up in. Besides being a keen observer of nature he was an indefatigable keeper of pets—jackdaws, geese, frogs and toads, sticklebacks and small fishes of many kinds, snakes, lizards, mice, voles, shrews, and squirrels—all were welcome. So Konrad fits in beautifully with the pattern we have already seen well established as typical of the pioneers of ethology, as having started as an amateur naturalist at an early age. In fact with Konrad the real basis for his central contribution to zoology must have been laid exceptionally early. From the beginning he was fascinated by the concept of instinct, realised that it was little understood, and began dimly to see how the components which made up this mysterious and indefinable entity could be disentangled and ultimately investigated scientifically. He once told me that he feels that all the more important things he now knows about animal behaviour he already 'knew' by the time he was sixteen. As readers of that delightful book *King Solomon's Ring* will know, Konrad's particular forte was the raising of both wild and domestic animals by hand, living with them at the closest quarters and so gaining the first insights into the relation between the inherited aspects of their behaviour and the elements which are modified by early experience. Konrad trained as a medical student at the University of Vienna, and this was followed by further periods of specialization in comparative anatomy, psychology, and philosophy.

Konrad's father had a consulting clinic in the United States which took him almost yearly to that country, and he was sometimes accompanied by his son. As a result of this Konrad stayed for a two-semester stint in the Columbia Medical School in New York in 1922 and even there he is said to have spent more time studying the inhabitants of the New York aquarium than in attending medical lectures. Following his father he in due course completed his full qualifications in medicine at the University of Vienna, then becoming what we should call 'a part time Demonstrator' in anatomy and later Lecturer in Comparative Anatomy and Animal Psychology.

But all the time Konrad was continuing his naturalistic observations on pet animals at his Altenberg home where in fact all his early observations (1931–41) were made. During this time he was also in close contact with the great German ornithologist Oskar Heinroth who was already using the term 'ethology' for these naturalistic studies (a term which he seems very clearly to have taken over from Alfred Giard and/or Henri Fabre). He has always acknowledged Heinroth as 'his teacher' but he also pays tribute in the second of this series of papers to the influence of Jakob von Uexküll; the paper in question being dedicated to the latter on his seventieth birthday.

During the period 1931–41 Lorenz produced eight substantial papers which established the bounds of the discipline of ethology and largely determined the future course of ethological investigations for some twenty years. Of these eight, five are of outstanding importance and must be listed here. They are:

1. 'Beiträge zur Ethologie der sozialer Corviden', *Journal für Ornithologie*, 1931, **79**, 67–127.
2. 'Der Kumpan in der Umwelt des Vogels', *Journal für Ornithologie*, 1935, **83**, 137–214; 289–413.
3. 'Uber den Begriff der Instinkthandlung', *Folia Biotheoretica*, 1937, **2**, 17–50.

4. 'Vergleichende Verhaltensforschung', *Zoologische Anzeiger*, 1939, *Supplement* 12, 69–102.
5. 'Vergleichende Bewegungstudien an Anatinen', *Journal für Ornithologie*, 1941, **89** (*Erganzungsband* 3), 194–294.

It was the reading of these great papers that effected my own conversion from a student of insect physiology and parasitology to an ethologist, and I think that their effect on me may illustrate the development of thought I imagine must have taken place in many other naturalists when they first read them. The first four are now available in English translation.[2]

During the early 1940s I was becoming increasingly absorbed in, and puzzled by, what one may call the 'problem of instinct' and the relation of this to the learning abilities of animals. Yet the whole field seemed extraordinarily difficult. I had become progressively involved with the problem of instinct as exemplified by the behaviour of higher insects and birds, and Konrad's work threw what then seemed to me to be a powerful light on my own problems. For the physiological and psychological literature which I already knew fairly well had left me in the dark. Much of Konrad's work at this time was of course tentative and may appear to us now as unduly dogmatic. But his great achievement was to relate and synthesize all these problems into a single system of 'instincts' in such a way that I, at least, saw for the first time the key points at which further observation and experiment would be profitable—he produced order where there was previously chaos. A forthright and dogmatic approach was, I believe, exactly what was needed at that juncture and I consider that this is one of the basic reasons for his success as compared with the 'failure' of Wheeler and Lashley. When we feel critical today of Konrad's early papers it is important to remember, as Tinbergen has pointed out, that Lorenz explicitly wrote (I give Tinbergen's translation), 'I do not see any danger in formulating my (perhaps rather heretical) views in this provocative, extreme way as long as we are aware that they are working hypotheses and that we should be prepared to modify if new facts force us to do so. One thing, however, I hope and believe to have shown convincingly: that the investigation of instinctive behaviour is not a subject for grand metaphysical speculation, but, at least for the time being, a task to be pursued by concrete experimental analysis.'

I believe it is also important to show that the very fact that Lorenz's early papers now appear so outdated is a tribute to their effectiveness. If they were to appear now as satisfactory as they did then, it could only mean that they had failed in their object. It is the impetus that they gave to experimental work which has, in a sense, rendered them so quickly out of date, although they are of course still extremely well worth reading.

During the period of Konrad's life we have been discussing he married a childhood friend, Gretel Gebhardt, who was also a

Figure 8 Konrad Lorenz. Photographed in Cambridge, 1959.

medical student and who practised for many years as a consultant gynaecologist. It would be impossible here to go into the great help and inspiration that his marriage has been in his life, but one anecdote which Gretel tells will perhaps bear recounting. Once at a rather boring University party in Vienna, Gretel was beset by a tiresome young lady who had just made a very 'successful' marriage and who poured into her ear full details of how she met and fell in love with her husband and what a marvellous person he was. At last, apparently realising that she was monopolizing the conversation, she asked Gretel, 'And how did you meet your husband, Frau Lorenz?'. Gretel told her what was practically the truth, as follows: 'One day I was in my pram and I saw another pram coming along and in it was a great fat baby, and I said to myself, "That's him!" ' Gretel in fact came from the next village to Altenberg and the two constantly played together as children.

Although those who have read *King Solomon's Ring* will get a good impression of the Lorenz household there is one fascinating anecdote of definite biological interest which, though it appears in the original German version of the book, *Er redete mit dem Vieh, den Vogeln und den Fischen* (1949), was for some reason omitted from the English one. The Lorenzes had a pet grey lag goose named Martina. This goose slept in Konrad's bedroom and would fly out of the window in the morning to spend the day in the garden. At dusk it would be let in the front door and would walk up the stairs to bed. The main hall of the house, as is shown in Figure 9, has the front door at one end and a large window at the other. A broad staircase leads from the middle of the right side of the hall and curves around up to a gallery off which the bedrooms open. One evening just as Martina had come in, a door slammed and frightened her, upon which instead of going up the stairs she rushed towards the window, very nearly taking wing in the process. She had then to be pacified and coaxed upstairs to bed. Every night for some weeks after this the goose, apparently remembering its fright, would walk nearly to the window and then turn back and proceed up the middle of the broad staircase. With the passage of time this detour towards the window gradually decreased until all that was left of it was the curious habit of

(a)   (b)   (c)   (d)

Figure 9 Konrad Lorenz's goose Martina showing the development of a 'superstition'. (a) Martina's normal route upstairs to bed. (b) Martina, alarmed by the slamming of the hall door, rushes suddenly towards the window. (c) After some weeks the detour towards the window is gradually eliminated but is still made as a lingering result of the fright caused by the banging door. (d) Final route taken by Martina. She comes in straight towards the door, but does a sharp right turn to walk up the centre of the staircase. Drawings by Priscilla Barrett.

walking first towards the window, but when coming opposite the middle point of the stairway giving a sharp right turn and walking up the middle of the stairs. One evening the family forgot the goose which was left out in the garden until after dark; long after its normal bedtime. Then someone said, 'My goodness, we've forgotten the goose,' and went and opened the door. Martina, agitated and flustered, quickly started diagonally up the stairs at the point nearest the door, omitting the usual steps towards the window and the sudden right turn. She had gone up a few steps when she suddenly stopped in alarm and appeared about to take flight. Halting just in time she turned round, walked down the stairs to the exact middle point, then made the formal right turn—as if carrying out some propitiatory ritual; she then commenced to walk up the stairs in her normal manner. After having gone a few steps she stopped, 'greeted', shaking and settling her feathers as if to say, 'My goodness I nearly forgot the time', whereupon she went calmly upstairs to bed. It was as if the last remains of the ritual, the detour towards the window, had acquired a sort of superstitious value in some way associated with the awareness of the consequences of the one occasion on which she had been badly frightened. The use here of the word 'superstition' in fact corresponds very closely to its use by B. F. Skinner and other 'learning psychologists'.

During the period in question a flourishing and very forward-looking school of naturalists had come into being in Holland. They were primarily ornithologists and published their work in the Dutch bird journal *Ardea*. Some of them were amateurs and others professional, the two groups being fairly well balanced. In this respect Holland was ahead of Great Britain because at that time the study of birds by professional zoologists here was quite exceptional and it was left to the amateur to provide the foundation for the study of bird behaviour. To take the Dutch group roughly in chronological order, A. F. J. Portielje was active from 1921 and into the post-war period. He was a sound ethologist of his period, working on birds and many other animals. While he helped to set the scene for ethological studies in Holland, and although his papers contain much of interest, particularly in relation to the display of sexual and social releasers, he delayed publishing his theoretical ideas—which seem to have been of real significance—until late in life when he produced a voluminous book on animal behaviour written in Dutch. Many English naturalists were keen to have this translated and the Association for the Study of Animal Behaviour made considerable efforts to arrange for the publication of an English edition. However the result of enquiries of several Dutch naturalists and zoologists was that though interesting and in its way important the author's style was so extraordinary as to be virtually untranslatable! Evidently in this respect another Edmund Selous! But there is no doubt that Portielje's outstanding gifts, amounting indeed to genius, were displayed as Director of the Amsterdam Zoo. He was a man of commanding presence and powerful voice; altogether a tremendous personality. He once spent two or three hours taking me round his Zoological Gardens. It was an experience I shall never forget. He seemed to know all the animals personally and their response to him was quite extraordinary. He trumpeted to an elephant right across the gardens and got an immediate response.

He went into the hippopotamus house, whereupon the hippo surfaced and opened its mouth in order to experience the apparently delicious sensation of having its palate gently scratched. Similarly a rhinoceros squatted and managed to look sentimental. We came to the lionhouse where there was a big male sitting closely against the bars. Portielje put his hand through and stroked the lion on the side of the face; getting in return a very slight raising of the lips into a snarl. Portielje said to me, 'It's my fault; you see, his lioness is on that side and that makes him slightly jealous. If I had done it on the other side of the face it would have been quite all right.' And so it went on. I particularly remember the delight which his appearance caused to a leopard who rolled about in ecstasy on seeing him. Portielje said he often went into the cage and romped with him, but in order to do that he had to put on special clothes or otherwise it became too expensive and messy. In fact one wonders if there has ever been a better Zoo director; and seeing him with his animals made one feel that however difficult a translation of his book may have seemed in prospect, it might nevertheless have proved worthwhile even if only partially intelligible.

Another Dutchman who was highly thought of at one time was J. A. Bierens de Haan. He accomplished much interesting observational work on such subjects as tool-using, the problem of number concept in animals, colour sense and mental capacities of the octopus, and the analysis of bird display. But he was a comparative psychologist who did not take very kindly to ethological ideas. In 1940 he produced a large book on animal instinct and its development through experience (*Die Tierischen Instinkte und ihr Umbau durch Erfahrung*), which was a distinctive and valuable source of material. Yet it showed the defect, not uncommon among pre-ethological naturalists, of too readily despairing of the successful analysis of elaborate examples of instinctive behaviour. He tended to regard instincts as something ultimate in the animal's behaviour and so the result of his work was often to discourage, rather than to promote, a deeper study of the subject

Another very fine observer was G. F. Makkink, who in the mid 1930s and 1940s made a remarkable attempt at a full ethogram of the European avocet (*Recurvirostra avocetta*) and the oyster-catcher (*Haematopus ostralegus*). Also outstanding was the work of Jan Verwey who in 1929–30 published splendid studies on the ethology of the heron (*Ardea cinerea*). But perhaps the most notable example on these lines (excluding Niko Tinbergen) was that of A. Kortlandt whose work on the European cormorant (*Phalacrocorax carbo*)—published in Dutch in 1938 and in German two years later—was outstanding and led him to make invaluable analyses of the concept of displacement activities and *Übersprungbewegung*: a term which later became familiar in English as 'sparking-over'.

I think it important to go into such detail concerning this remarkable group of Dutch workers since they formed the milieu in which Niko Tinbergen developed; he would I am sure be the first to acknowledge his indebtedness to them, for he was able to build so successfully on some of the foundations which they laid.

So we come to Niko Tinbergen himself. Tinbergen's earliest papers were on birds. Notable among them were those dealing with the common tern (*Sterna hirundo*) and his early observations on gulls. Since the publications of Verwey (referred to above) preceded those of Tinbergen it is reasonable to suppose that he was a good deal influenced by them. But by the time the second paper on terns was published (1932) he had already been working for some time on the habits and behaviour of the fossorial wasps; his fine studies on the bee-hunting digger wasp, *Philanthus triangulum*, saw the light that same year. The first of these papers were on homing behaviour, the second in 1935 on hunting behaviour, an outstanding study followed in 1938 on the selective learning of landmarks. Such behavioural work on insects had not been much favoured by Dutch experimentalists, but after that date it can be assumed that the influence between Niko and his experimental confederates, such as Makkink and Kortlandt, was, while still mutual, increasingly from him to them. With regard to his insect work it seems quite clear that, as far as it was influenced by the work of others, it came first from Karl von Frisch and some of the German and French workers; but later Mathilde

Hertz played a considerable role. A daughter of the discoverer of the Hertzian waves, Mathilde produced striking and important papers on the organisation of the visual field in bees and on physiology of the perception of movement. Her early papers were much influenced by concepts of the Gestalt psychologists. This added to the complexity of an already involved German style which many foreigners found difficult to comprehend—but when understood it is extremely rewarding. She left Germany in the early days of the Jewish exodus and came to Cambridge where she worked in the Department of Zoology for some time under Dr A. D. Imms. However, when the war actually erupted she was much distressed; though forced to be an exile from Nazism her love for her native land was immensely strong and before long she felt the world antipathy to her own country harder and harder to bear—even though realising full well the justification for it. At length the situation became intolerable for her and so she retired more and more into herself until very much a recluse. She still lives in Cambridge but has long broken all her scientific contacts.

As a Zoology student at Leiden, Niko Tinbergen had not impressed his Professors overmuch—largely because of his pre-occupation with sport, which included skating, pole jumping, and hockey, the latter to International standards. Fortunately things went the right way (although perhaps the wrong way from the point of view of Dutch hockey!) in that he became steadily more fascinated by the behaviour of insects and birds. Right at the beginning he showed both acute powers of observation and the immense patience required to produce an almost complete inventory of the various behaviour patterns of gestures and actions employed by the animal he was studying, whether it was a hunting wasp, a snow bunting, or a falcon. This ability was basic. But Niko went far beyond this in his remarkable powers of devising simple field experiments and in finding simple problems which he could put to his animals in the wild without disturbing them unduly. This yielded deep insights into their powers of perception and would show the extent to which they were able to cope with and overcome new problems which he would set them—such as moving a conspicuous landmark (a twig, a plant, or a pine cone) near a hunting wasps' nest.

By great good fortune he had been able to spend a year in the Scoresby Sound region of East Greenland as a member of a small Dutch expedition which also included four young but highly experienced British explorers, Gino Watkins, Freddy Chapman, John Rymill, and Quentin Riley. The invitation to do this came suddenly just as Niko was preoccupied in putting in his thesis for the Doctorate of Philosophy and moreover getting engaged to be married! His typical irrepressibility and panache solved these two little problems successfully. First—by rushing through his thesis (fortunately without deleterious results) and secondly by arranging for his fiancée to come with him to Greenland. The arrangement was a tremendous success and beautiful field studies of snow buntings, phalaropes, and Eskimo dogs resulted. These early studies set the pattern for his life's work and showed him to be the very incarnation of the ethological ideal. His papers up to and including the year 1937, while ultimately of great theoretical value, did not themselves give much space to theoretical problems. In 1938 Konrad Lorenz invited Niko to work with him at his home at Altenberg and this resulted in a crucially important year together. Konrad had the insight to realise that not being primarily an experimentalist himself he needed the attitude of mind that a gifted experimenter would bring to his field, and nowhere could he have found a better complement than in Niko. Their joint paper on the egg-rolling movements of the nesting goose combining taxis with instinctive action is famous. Then in 1939 Niko published his classic paper jointly with D. J. Kuenen on the releasing and directing stimuli of the gaping response in young blackbirds and thrushes. But not until his 1939 paper did he quote any of the five great papers of Konrad Lorenz discussed above.

The collaboration with Lorenz was rudely shattered with the coming of the war and the war fortunes or misfortunes of these two will be traced later. In 1940 Tinbergen was also able to publish his classic work on displacement activities, and an important theoretical paper in 1942, *An Objective Study of the Innate Behavior of Animals*.[3]

Konrad has a delightful story of an occasion during Niko's 1938 stay in Vienna. The two had been into the city and were sitting in the restaurant of the Nordbahnhof drinking coffee while they were waiting for their train. Meanwhile two young ladies whose intention was only too obvious came and seated themselves at a nearby table. Niko turned to Konrad and said loudly, 'QUACK quack-quack-quack-quack, QUACK quack-quack-quack-quack.' This in fact is the call given by the mallard duck when she wants to attract the attentions of a drake. On hearing it the two ladies rose and left hurriedly with every appearance of alarm and astonishment.

In 1940 Konrad was appointed a full Professor of the University of Königsberg in East Prussia. This was partly in recognition of his knowledge of psychology and behaviour and also, it seems, in appreciation of his wide knowledge of philosophy, particularly that of Kant. It was thought at that time that Konrad's work was particularly relevant to Kant's ideas and that the appointment was appropriate to a University where Kant had himself been a Professor. Not long after Konrad was installed as a professor he heard that Niko had been sent to a hostage camp in Holland. He tried his utmost, in concert with Otto Köhler, to secure his release—but in vain.

Some time in 1943 when the position of the German army on the East Front was beginning to appear critical, Konrad was withdrawn from his Professorship and was directed into the Army Medical Service as Consultant Psychiatrist. Shortly after this, it happened that Goering discovered that one of the most famous German fighter pilots had at an early stage in his career been classified by the psychiatric service as unfit for combatant duty. The Field Marshal was so incensed by this that he instantly erased the Psychiatric Service with a stroke of his pen.

Konrad's superiors in the department of military psychology told him that it would be some six months before this edict filtered down to Konrad's relatively lowly level. They added that though there would be nothing for him to do he must nevertheless come to the office every day until the group was finally disbanded. So Konrad, presented with a period of about six months official idleness, occupied himself by writing a considerable scientific paper. At the end of that time he was drafted into the German Army as an ordinary Medical Officer and sent to the Eastern Front. He tells us that it was not until he reached Poland that he began to realise the full horror of the Nazi system and its treatment of the subjugated peoples.

In 1944 the Russians had driven the German armies right back to the region of Vitebsk and to the line of the Dniester and of Odessa, thus liberating the whole of the Crimea and nearly all the rest of the eastern areas previously captured. In June of this year Konrad found himself involved in the savage fighting behind the Russian lines at Vitebsk. He was captured by the Russians and though slightly wounded managed to escape immediately. Then he and a comrade rushed towards the opposite lines with their hands up shouting, 'Don't shoot, we're Germans.' However at that stage, at the height of the battle, two Russian groups were fighting one another, as we suppose may often happen under such conditions. So Konrad merely landed up as a captive of another Russian unit.

He received sympathetic treatment at the hands of his captors and, being a magnificent linguist, he soon learned Russian and was further distinguished in that he went about with a pet starling on his shoulder. The Russians, sensibly taking advantage of his medical knowledge, then sent him down to the newly liberated Crimea and in due course placed him in charge of a small Military Prisoner of War hospital.

Conditions there were severe and they were often short of food. But the whole population was in the same plight: food was stolen on the way to its destination and in fact there seems to have been no evidence that the prisoners were any worse off than were the native inhabitants of the area.

After he was established in his hospital the rate of capture of prisoners waned and there was often very little for the hospital to do; so Konrad started surreptitiously to write a book he had long had in mind, a general encyclopaedic work on animal behaviour. He acquired the paper somehow, scrounging it where necessary and always hiding away the manuscript when anyone came in. From time to time warnings came that the hospital was going to be inspected by some general or other high official. These inspections never materialized with the result that Konrad became rather blasé about it all. Then one day a message came to say that a real Minister was coming to inspect the hospital. Konrad said to his orderlies, 'I don't believe any longer in these visits by the great men. Tidy up the front of the hospital, I shall go on working here quietly in my office at the back.' Of course that time, as would happen, a real Minister materialized and to Konrad's astonishment, opened the door and put his head round the door saying to Konrad, 'Well, what are you doing?'. Konrad leapt to attention and said, 'Er . . . er . . . I'm writing a book, Sir.' 'What about?' 'Animal behaviour.' 'Oh, like Pavlov.' In fact the work was not at all like Pavlov, but Konrad said, 'Er . . . er . . . Yes, like Pavlov.' Whereupon the Minister said, 'Oh, isn't that a good idea,' and immediately gave an order to the effect that this man might in future have all his time for writing his book, and need do no other duties! And as the war went on, wherever he went, this order followed him, so powerful was the edict of this particular Minister.

At length the war ended and after a long delay the time came for repatriation. By then the work had grown very large and Konrad asked whether he would be allowed to take the book out with him. This was a question beyond the competence of local commanders and had to be referred to Moscow. After some weeks the answer came back, Yes, he could take the book out with him provided he was willing to be transferred to a prisoner of war camp in Moscow and type out a copy to be left in the Russian Academy of Sciences Library. And in all the turmoil in Russia after the end of the war this was done, transfer to Moscow was arranged, he was given a typewriter, the book was typed out, a copy was initialled by a General who didn't look at it and Konrad returned to Altenberg with his book.

Soon after he returned Konrad made arrangements for publication; but since the book had been written entirely from memory (and his memory is truly phenomenal) it would have needed complete re-writing especially in view of the fact that the author had been cut off from all scientific literature for many years; particularly the literature on animal learning produced by the

American schools of comparative psychology during that period. I arranged to send Konrad some of the key writings, or at least summaries of them. But the task of re-writing proved too great and the book unfortunately (or perhaps fortunately) never saw the light; effective re-writing might even have been impossible at that time.

During his absence Altenberg had been occupied by Russian officers and Konrad's own father had stayed on there and established agreeable relations with the Russians. During the latter part of her husband's captivity Gretel had left Altenberg and taken the family to the western part of Austria, the Voralberg; at that time Gretel was quite uncertain as to Konrad's fate. She was back in the house with the family soon after the war ended and in spite of all the strains and anxieties which had taken toll of both of them, the atmosphere was wonderfully happy and contented—apart from some severe anxieties about the children's health after the deprivations of war.

However there is a little postscript to the sad story of the book which is worth telling. The Russians of course had a broadcasting system in their zone of Vienna for regular dissemination of information in the German language. Konrad's son, who was a competent radio fan, arranged, at a time when the family were normally listening to the Russian broadcast, to substitute a record imitating the accent and speech of the Russian announcer which said, 'We are now going to broadcast extracts from a remarkable book by Professor Konrad Lorenz, now once again living in Vienna', and started off with an extract. The shock was overwhelming and it was some minutes before they realised what had happened.

At the end of the war Niko Tinbergen was released from the hostage camp; in 1946 contacts between Dutch and British biologists became possible and it was from this date that our close personal friendship developed. But there was still no news of Lorenz; rumour had it that he was dead. But then in 1948 came the joyful tidings that far from being dead he was back in his home in Altenberg. I immediately made contact and went to Vienna in that year at his pressing invitation. There were some difficulties in that Altenberg was in the Russian zone but these were fortunately overcome. Our talk ranged widely over zoology, ornithology, physiology, Pavlovian dogmatics, psychology, and of course, above all, ethology and every conceivable excursion from these topics—grave and gay, tragic and comic. So I shall always remember vividly the inexpressibly stimulating and delightful few days that I spent with Konrad and Gretel in Altenberg.

I was fortunate too in that J. B. Priestley and his wife (now Mrs D. A. Bannerman), hearing of Konrad's return and realising that the then desperate conditions still prevailing in Vienna must be creating appalling problems for Konrad's little 'Institute' (which in fact was still the house and grounds of his childhood home), asked me to try to arrange, when in Vienna, for the royalties which had accumulated (as a result mainly of the performance of Priestley's plays there) to be transferred to Konrad's Institute. This I was happily able to do and it is this that explains the charming dedication on the title page of *King Solomon's Ring*—that it is thanks to Mr and Mrs J. B. Priestley that the jackdaws still fly over Altenberg.

Another urgent reason for my visit to Altenberg was to make further arrangements for a conference in Cambridge the next year. In 1947 the British Society for Experimental Biology had organised a very successful conference in Utrecht together with their opposite numbers in Holland and several of us, including Niko Tinbergen and a number of members of the British Association for the Study of Animal Behaviour (A.S.A.B.) arranged that the Society for Experimental Biology and the A.S.A.B. should join forces in organising a truly international conference in 1949 on the topic 'Physiological Mechanisms in Animal Behaviour'. I think that we can claim that this marked the beginning of real international co-operation between ethologists. It is safe to say that none present at this conference will fail to remember it for the rest of his life. But for us personally it remains particularly vivid because of a moving event, namely the reunion in our house in Cambridge of Niko and Konrad after a separation of almost exactly ten years. The 1949 conference included representatives from Britain, Holland, Austria, Germany, Poland, and the USA.

Here I must refer to one particular outcome of the conference. Unfortunately Erich von Holst was unable to attend. Soon afterwards he wrote inviting several of us to visit his laboratory in Wilhelmshaven—The Max-Planck-Institüt für Verhaltens-physiologie (then part of the M.P.I. für Meeresbiologie)—for ten days during the following year. This small but extremely lively gathering was as memorable as its predecessor. Apart from myself and Niko Tinbergen (whom I 'picked up' on my way through Holland) all were from Germany and Austria. They included Konrad Lorenz (by this time with the Max-Planck Institüt), Otto Koehler, Gustav Kramer, Wolfgang Metzger, Ursula von Saint Paul, Laura Schoen, and last but not least two brilliantly promising research students of Erich's—Bernard Hassenstein and Horst Mittelstaedt.

The conditions at Wilhelmshaven were curious and incon-venient. The Max-Planck Institüt was housed in a newly con-structed but unfinished naval barracks building, rendered vacant by the liquidation of the Wilhelmshaven naval establishment after the war. The quarters were cramped; with the staff and students living closely packed. In spite of this the relationship between the forthright, dominating, and difficult von Holst and his students intrigued me. While the students clearly revered their Professor, their conversation with him being at times highly formal and deferential, there was nevertheless alongside this a family atmos-phere as of promising children with their parents. For the students seemed able to drop in on the von Holsts at almost any hour of the day or night for help or conversation; and sometimes the exchanges were quite vigorous. I recall one between two of the research workers on the one hand and von Holst and Otto Koehler on the other, which ended with the latter being called a silly old man (or words to that effect!). I expected an explosion: for though Otto resembled a kindly yet pedantic old schoolmaster he was also one of the most distinguished research workers in animal behaviour in the country and moreover was the 'doyen' of German zoologists. This meant that in the last resort he had almost overwhelming power, through his advisory relations with the State, over all zoological posts and departments in the country and was most certainly not a man one would carelessly antagonize. This was shown by the fact that even Konrad Lorenz seemed slightly 'afraid' of him and somewhat subdued in his company. But, astonishingly enough, there was no explosion and all passed off serenely. Perhaps the ease of social relations in this small scientific community owed much to Frau von Holst; a tall and beautiful Swedish girl who, like a great and graceful tree, spread a shade of stillness and peace. Erich's debt to her must have been incalculable.

The conference was ideal and (most befitting in a small group) striking for its lack of organisation. There was no set programme and no regular 'chairperson'. Soon after arrival I was asked if I would give a talk the next day. I was somewhat shocked when my query as to how long I should speak for produced the reply, 'Oh! about two hours'. But this was because questions, interpolations, and comments occurred continually throughout: somewhat disconcerting at first, though quite a good plan when a small well-knit group has ample time for all to have their say. The only rule which I remember Erich laying down for the proceedings was that the talks must be informal and confidential reports on work in progress. '*Nur halb-gelegt Eier*,' as he said. (Only half-laid eggs.)

Niko Tinbergen's attitude at this gathering deserves a special word; for the memories of the German occupation of his country and above all of the years in the hostage camp were still very vividly in his mind. So much so that when our train crossed the border from Holland on our way to Wilhelmshaven he found the sound of German being talked in the train and in the streets an almost unendurable reminder of the occupation. Yet though this was an uncontrollable psychological response it affected his relations with individual German friends and colleagues at the conference not a whit: most remarkable evidence of the depth and strength of his desire for international reconciliation at all levels.

So, thanks to Erich von Holst, this Wilhelmshaven gathering was the forerunner of the long series of International Ethological Conferences which have continued at two-yearly intervals ever since. It has also set the standard for the style of gathering to be aimed at—not less than ten days duration, small, confidential, informal, and by personal invitation: a style which has been maintained as far as the immense increase in the number of workers and range of topics over the years have permitted.

REFERENCES

1. Gould, J. L., 'Honey bee recruitment: the dance language controversy', *Science*, 1975, **189**, 685–93.
2. Schiller, C. H. (Editor), *Instinctive Behaviour: the development of a modern concept* (London: Methuen, 1957).
3. Tinbergen, N., 'An objectivistic study of the innate behaviour of animals', *Bibliotheca Biotheoretica*, 1942, **1**, 39–98.

Part II

THE RISE OF ETHOLOGY

6

The conceptual system at 1950: key topics and attitudes

In Part I the development of ethology up to the year 1950 has been outlined. I now wish to attempt documentation and explanation of the tremendous, indeed almost explosive, growth undergone by the science of the study of natural behaviour of animals in the early years of the following decade. To do this we must survey some of the key topics and attitudes in the biology and psychology of the period upon which the ethological approach effected such far-reaching transformations.

The first and in many ways most basic topic scrutinized was that of 'instinct' and the motivation or drive (physiological and/or psychological) which underlies it.

The wonderfully complex and seemingly purposive behaviour of many kinds of relatively lowly animals such as spiders and ants has amazed and entranced mankind since at least the days when the Book of Proverbs was written. Behaviour of the kind characteristic of such creatures has for long been known as 'instinctive'— derived from the Latin *instinctus* (incited or instigated). Besides its use for animals it has in recent centuries often been applied to the compelling and little understood factors that incite or drive human behaviour; and indeed so-called human instincts have sometimes been regarded as substantially emotional and this tinges and complicates the general use of the word at the present day. The word originally meant 'driven from within'.

The naturalists of the second half of the nineteenth century tended to use the term in an extremely vague manner. Because they were primarily interested in animals in the field rather than the laboratory or dissecting room, and because they were particularly involved with systematics, life history, geographical distribution, etc., they contributed little to this aspect of the study of behaviour as a scientific discipline. Unfortunately the work of the physiologists and the great majority of contemporary psychologists was almost equally useless—the great contributions of William James and William McDougall being then underestimated. For a long time physiologists had been employing the concept of reflex action—by which they denoted the simple and almost invariable response of a simple organ system (ideally a single muscle) to a simple stimulus (e.g. a touch, a flash of light, or a slight electric shock). In this way the concept of the reflex arc arose, and towards the end of the nineteenth century the physiological view of animal behaviour was primarily that of the co-ordination of a very large number of these simple, quick, muscular movements executed as an immediate response to simple environmental stimuli and to combinations of such stimuli in various degrees of complexity. It was thus fashionable to suppose that this was the basic element of behaviour and that all the more complex behaviour patterns could be regarded as what were called chain-reflexes; motions such those as of walking, swallowing, and so forth, being constituted by one reflex setting off another and so producing complex, fairly stereotyped, and highly co-ordinated movements. Thus the physiologists of the time would have said that instinctive actions are nothing but elaborate chain-reflexes.

To biologists and naturalists concerned with the overall study of the behaviour of animals, this explanation seemed to be facile and incomplete. So, while instincts were seen as a fact of the life of animals, there was virtually no effective theory as to how they were brought about, how organised or how developed. We must therefore start by considering the various more elementary ideas about animal movements, and how it was that these, by themselves, did not carry the scientific analysis of instinctive behaviour very far. Although the concept of instinct had remained confused and difficult until towards the middle of the twentieth century, scientific studies of the way in which the lower animals are able to direct their movements so as to be sure of finding the essential goals of their existence (e.g., the right intensities of light, temperature, humidity, etc.) and so find food, shelter, and members of the opposite sex, had been undertaken much earlier. That is to say zoologists had already made big advances in understanding how lower animals find their way about their environment. So it was that many useful concepts and terms had been established before 1930—notably by A. Kuhn (1914–29) and Jacques Loeb (1913).

The terms in use in this early and highly successful phase of the study of animal behaviour described, first, the elementary physiological concepts employed, and secondly the concepts particularly related to the steering of the whole animal. In the first group we have: (a) REFLEX: *an innate relatively simple and stereotyped response involving the central nervous system and occurring very shortly after the stimulus which provokes it. It specifically involves a part only of the organism,* though the whole may be affected; and is usually a response to localized sensory stimuli. (b) INHIBITION: this was such a standard physiological term that it seemed not to require a precise definition for use in ethology. But it was thought by ethologists of the period that the term should, as far as possible, be employed in the original physiological sense of Sherrington as implying the competition of two behaviour patterns for the same mechanism or situations where the interaction of the two behaviour patterns produces a reduction in the intensity of some feature of them. (c) FACILITATION: here again we have a term which was of clear meaning and value in physiology but not often specifically required in the description of behaviour and which was therefore restricted, as far as possible, to physiological uses. (d) INERTIA: this term was originally introduced into behaviour studies to mean 'the time required to change from mood to mood', for instance, the time taken by an organism such as a fish to change from fighting to courting behaviour. While the term was undoubtedly useful in this sense, once again it was a word in common and well understood usage with a precise physical meaning and therefore should be understood in behaviour studies as a metaphor only.

Now we come to terms particularly valuable for the description and analysis of locomotory movements and behaviour associated therewith.

The first and simplest kind of locomotory behaviour is what is called KINESIS. In this there is no orientation of the body relative to the source of stimulation. That is to say the animal has not the sensory powers to guide it directly towards a stimulus, for example a sound or light. There are many subdivisions of this category of kinesis, but the term as a whole can be defined as *locomotory behaviour not involving a steering reaction but in which there may be turning, random in direction.* For instance, *orthokinesis* (the rate of movement) and *klinokinesis* (the amount of turning) are related to the intensity of stimulation. To mention one example, woodlice (*Oniscus asellus*) are very sensitive to drying out since their skin is not well waterproofed, so they have to remain in air of high humidity if they are to keep alive. If a woodlouse is placed in a chamber in which the humidity is controlled, one finds that, other things being equal, it walks more slowly when in the higher humidity and faster if the air is dry. In nature this means that woodlice will tend to aggregate in the damper places since they will slow up there. *Orthokinesis* is a good term for this behaviour in that the animal does not necessarily need to wheel to the right or left nor is it necessarily capable of doing so. All it need do is change its rate of walking.

A more important kind of kinesis is *klinokinesis*. This phenomenon is shown very beautifully by flatworms (*Dendrocoelum*) when crawling about on the bottom of a flat glass dish of water, one end of which is more highly illuminated than the other but with diffuse *indirect* lighting. In this situation we find that, although the animals do not seem to be consistently walking in any one direction, they nevertheless all end up at the darker end of the dish in due course. Investigations show that with a given temperature they all have a given *rate of change of direction.* That is to say that in a given time they all make a predictable average number of turns, totalling a given angular amount of turning, but indiscriminately to the right and left. At the start of the experiment it is found that those worms which are in the more intense light show a higher probability of turning. In this situation central adaptation of the light receptors to intensity of the light occurs fairly rapidly. A given light intensity therefore induces a higher probability of turning in an animal not yet adapted to that intensity and moving up the gradient than it does in one moving down the gradient, which has already started to become adapted to even higher intensities. The result of this is that the path of the worms tends to the darker regions, since such paths tend to be longer than paths away from the dark. Paths which expose the animals to gradually increasing light intensity result in their again turning more, thus aggregating in the dark. This is because the rate of turning decreases with decreasing stimulation (see Figure 10a). In such an experiment, partly because the light-sensitive organs of the flatworms only perceive intensity but not direction, and partly because of the conditions of the experiment, it is quite impossible for the worm to orientate itself towards the light. Figure 10b shows the same sort of behaviour in response to a chemical stimulus diffusing or spreading out uniformly in all directions from a given centre. It is very well seen in animals such as lice, e.g. the human louse (*Pediculus humanus*). For with a given 'attractive' physical substance, the rate of turning decreases with an increase in intensity of stimulation. The result is that the animal tends to walk straighter when increasing its sensory stimulation and more crookedly when moving away from it—with the inevitable result that it ends up at the source of the odour.

Next we consider locomotory behaviour involving a steering reaction. Such reactions are known as TAXES. These are reactions where orientation of the body with respect to the source of stimulation is attained. So we have *klinotaxis* where the animal still does not need to have sense organs discriminating direction of stimulation but only discriminating intensity. Thus a fly maggot swings its body from side to side, comparing intensities of light on different sides at successive instants. This enables it to approach a source of light even though (unless perhaps very close) it has no means of detecting the direction from which the light is coming. Klinotaxis is in fact rare to light because if animals get as far as developing eyes they usually soon reach the stage of having eyes that respond to direction *as well as* intensity. Klinotaxis is more

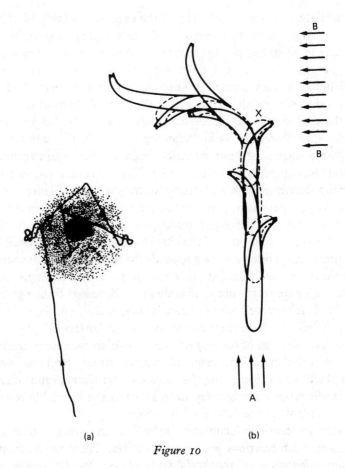

(a)   (b)

Figure 10

usual to chemical stimuli. Thus planarian worms seeking food may start with the convoluted path of klinokinesis then, as they get nearer the stimulus, one may see that the worms swing the front of their bodies from side to side just as the blow-fly maggot does, comparing intensities successively.

Tropotaxis is shown in animals with paired sense organs which are far enough apart and sufficiently sensitive to allow *simultaneous comparison* of intensities. This means that they do not have to swing from side to side but can go straight; a beetle or a wasp walking towards a light is able with its two eyes to compare intensity registered by the two sense organs continuously and simultaneously. Coming to more complicated means of orientation we have *telotaxis* which does not depend upon a simple balance of stimulation. In this case the animal can 'choose' one *or* other of two sources. It can inhibit the response of the sense organ on one side and direct itself towards the stiumlation of the other. Quite simply, one can say it no longer behaves like the proverbial donkey between two bales of hay but 'makes up its mind' that it will go to one or the other.

Then comes *menotaxis*, sometimes called the 'light compass reaction'. Here the animal can not only move to or away from the stimulus but can also maintain a constant angle towards it. This is very well shown by ants which are able to maintain a particular track from, say, their nest to foraging ground by keeping the sun at a definite angle to the axis of the body. From recent work on ants it looks as if this menotaxis is an acquired method super-imposed upon the pre-existing tropotactic response.

Finally there is *mnemotaxis*. This kind of orienting response can be shown only by animals which have eyes sufficiently well developed to detect a pattern or configuration. And this process of detecting a pattern or configuration naturally leads us straight into more complex theories concerning the way in which the initial stimuli received by the eyes are organised in the central nervous system. We find clear examples of mnemotaxis in such insects as hunting wasps and honey bees where there is extremely precise and accurate recognition of visual pattern as a result of experience. In this case, the animal, like ourselves, is able to choose one pattern rather than another and take a planned course towards it.

The study of controlled and directed movements was enormously advanced by the kinesis-taxis classification described above. It was useful not only for purposes of description and classification but also for relating the nature of the orientational responses to the complexity of the sensory equipment and so helped in considera-tions of their phylogeny. But valuable as this system was and still is, it has its dangers in that, though of admirable utility when employed in the laboratory under simply controlled conditions, it may simplify unduly and incorrectly the nature of the response of an animal under its normal conditions of life. For while the kinesis-taxis classification is perfectly applicable, many of the more active and highly organised animals have control systems of immense sophistication associated with their sense organs which enable them to analyse and compare the processes of stimulation and so bring their behaviour to an altogether higher level of organisation. An extreme example of this is the communication of the distance and direction of a food source by the honey bee when giving indications of the sun's bearing by its dance on a vertical comb surface (see Figure 7, page 63). Examples of still more elaborate and sophisticated methods employed for the purpose of orientation are provided by the long distance flights undertaken by birds during migration or homing.

So although work of this type was immensely valuable, and still is, it did not in the early decades of the century by itself provide any substantial help in the understanding of instinct—although once modern theories of instinct had been developed, the kinesis-taxis approach proved of value for the further detailed elucidation of the niceties of instinctive behaviour.

In the early decades of the present century the concept of instinct was so vague as to be ineffective as a stimulus to further investigation, and was the cause of conflicts which generated more heat than light. On the one hand there was the physiological approach which found its fullest expression in the work of Bethe, Loeb, and Pavlov. On the other hand there were the psychologists, stimulated by Darwin's *The Expression of Emotions in Man and Animals* with its essential and primarily psychological outlook. This group was impressed by the extreme complexity of instinct and the striking evidences of emotion which animals often display, and so the psychological approach to the study developed more or less independently of the other school. Both parties did very valuable work but although their two rapidly diverging viewpoints remained uneasily yoked in all comprehensive definitions of instinct, the combination was quickly becoming unmanageable. It was certainly made worse by the very vague, if not meaningless, use of the term 'instinct' in everyday speech. The natural outcome of all this was that the physiological school attempted to throw out the concept altogether, with stimulating attempts to describe all behaviour in terms of chain-reflexes, kineses, and taxes. The second school concentrated more and more on the modifiable aspects of behaviour and eventually became absorbed in experiments with cats in puzzle-boxes and rats in mazes and so developed a form of 'comparative psychology' which became increasingly devoted to the study of learning and less and less 'comparative', until the casual reader, coming fresh to the subject, might have been led to conclude that the only animals in existence were the white rat and the cat! One such worker (Kuo, in 1930) even reached the point of claiming that the assumption that there are inborn behaviour patterns in animals is quite unnecessary; though to do him justice he later withdrew from this extreme position and greatly extended the range of species upon which he worked.

Nevertheless, during a considerable part of this period the moderates of the two schools could no doubt have agreed on some points. In 1924 a compromise of this kind was achieved by G. E. Müller[1] who stated that 'instinct is an inherited psychophysical disposition whereby animals pay attention to particular objects or objects in a particular setting, and display a conative urge to perform complete, complex and often highly stereotyped actions in connection therewith.' This was a fairly comprehensive definition and it included three valuable points of agreement, (a) that instincts are inherited; (b) that they are usually complex; and (c) that they are often invoked by complex environmental situations (for example gestalts) in contrast to reflexes, kineses, and taxes which are characteristically evoked by simple stimuli.

Such briefly was the impasse reached when Konrad Lorenz, in his papers of 1937–39, produced in its definitive form a theory of instinctive behaviour which, although owing much to the work of the early workers in America and to his teacher Heinroth, was essentially new.[2]

Lorenz argued that in each example of instinctive behaviour there is a hard core of absolutely fixed, more or less complex, automatism—an inborn movement-form. This restricted concept is the *instinctive movement (Erbkoordination)* of Lorenz; and these automatisms were thought of as the essential central element in the whole system of 'instinctive behaviour' of any animal. Lorenz stressed that such instincts or 'movement forms' are items of behaviour in every way as constant as anatomical structures and potentially just as valuable for systematic and phylogenetic studies. That such instincts are indeed of systematic value in a great many groups of animals has by now been overwhelmingly demonstrated—both by Lorenz himself and by his mentor Heinroth, working with birds, especially ducks—and long before Heinroth by many entomologists studying the elaborate behaviour of social insects such as ants, bees, and wasps.

This was particularly noticed by the great naturalists of the turn of the century and earlier (Perris, Perez, Fenton, and J-H. Fabre in France, Adlerz in Sweden) who first unravelled the amazing specificity of behaviour in the fossorial wasps and other Hymenoptera (see also the Americans, Plath on bumble bees and Petrunkewitsch on spiders). But, unlike birds, the hard external structures of insects provide such a wealth of easily observable minute characteristics for classification that it was hardly necessary to base classification *primarily* upon behavioural features.

Heinroth's great paper of 1910 on the ethology of the Anatidae was a seminal contribution and one may fairly claim that Heinroth was perhaps the first person to use the behaviour of birds to provide convincing evidence for their phylogeny. Heinroth was indeed one of the greatest ornithologists of his time and Lorenz once described ethology as the subject invented and taught by Heinroth. As we have seen in Part I, this was not in fact the case. The term 'ethology' was in use in very much its present-day sense upwards of a century before Heinroth wrote, and he himself did not invent either the term or the subject.

It had been everywhere assumed that instinctive behaviour depends on some internal drive, but Lorenz's particular contribution to this phase of the subject consisted of his concept of *'reaction-specific energy'*. This was an unfortunate term in many ways and was immediately and with reason attacked by neurophysiologists and others. That Lorenz was essentially right cannot be doubted; and indeed this is part of the very idea of drive included by definition under the older term 'conative urge'—as

Figure 11 Oskar Heinroth, 1933. Photograph kindly supplied
by his widow, Frau Heinroth.

employed by psychologists. Lorenz pointed out that each instinct
tends to build up a kind of specific tension in the central nervous
system and if the animal does not find itself in the appropriate
situation for that instinct to be released this reaction-specific
energy is 'dammed up'. The damming up process results in a
lowering of the threshold of stimuli effective for *releasing* that
particular instinctive activity. Furthermore he argued that if
continued long enough the tension may accumulate to the point at
which the instinct 'goes off' without any external stimulus at all,
as it were forcing its way out and giving rise to what he called
leerlaufreaktion (vacuum activity).

Of course, pure instinct in Lorenz's sense would be almost useless by itself. In his original statement the instinct was regarded only as the central hard core of instinctive behaviour. Even the simplest case of instinctive behaviour consists of much more than this hard core; it includes the whole system, often extremely complex, of taxes and reflexes which make up the *appetitive behaviour* (Wallace Craig, 1918), and which is modifiable by conditioning and by other types of learning. It is this basic appetitive drive (as a part of that instinct as a whole) which in its turn enables the animal to attain the goal for which the whole behaviour sequence is adapted.

This appetitive behaviour may simply be non-directed locomotion, as in the kineses discussed above; examples of which are the random burrowing in the soil of many insect larvae or the random swimming of filter-feeding animals. Over and above this they can show appetitive behaviour consisting of directed locomotion of simpler types (kinesis plus taxes) described above, innumerable examples of which are known to every zoologist in the oriented behaviour enabling animals to find a particular required food, a particular host for them to parasitize, or members of the other sex of their own species. When the appetitive behaviour has run its appropriate course and the animal reaches the 'goal', the appropriate instinctive behaviour is released by the stimulus or *releaser* which it there encounters. This releaser, in Lorenz's terminology, is effective because of the existence of a *'receptory correlate'*—a sensory organization within the animal which enables it to recognise it and to act appropriately. This receptory correlate or releaser mechanism can be completely innate and entirely unmodifiable by individual experience—as it must be in the cocoon making or pupation behaviour of many insect larvae; complex behaviour which only occurs once in the life cycle and without which the survival of the indivudial would be impossible. On the other hand in the higher animals the perception of the releaser can be to a lesser or greater extent adjusted and conditioned by experience so as to be adaptable to particular circumstances. So this conditioning of the receptory correlate can be effected by a simple and quick reflex adjustment; provided only that the animal has some sort of predisposition or tendency to recognise its mate or its prey, but needs the fine adjustment of experience for success.

In some cases in the higher animals the adjustment process may be very elaborate indeed and in the young of precocial birds the response may be the means of achieving a very characteristic form of adjustment known as *imprinting*. Actually this imprinting was originally regarded (unjustifiably as has since transpired) as a special kind of learning.

Finally this scheme of Lorenz's, as developed later by Tinbergen and Kortlandt, explains conveniently a whole series of otherwise puzzling and awkward facts grouped under the heading of *displacement activities*. A displacement activity can be defined as *an apparently irrelevant movement occurring when an animal is under the influence of a powerful drive but is at the same time in some way prevented from expressing the urge appropriately.*

This then gives us the essential features of Lorenz's contribution to the problem of instinct. It will be immediately obvious that it was supported by an immense quantity of observational data of quite a different order from that which reinforced any previous writings on instinctive behaviour; moreover its detail made possible for the first time the organised experimental attacks on many different facets of the essential 'problems of instinct'. It was in fact the most significant stimulus to the founding of the modern study of ethology. It was also the greatest single factor in the subsequent growth and organisation of the discipline. Before proceeding further perhaps we had better summarize the series of definitions approximately as given by a group of behaviour students from old and new world countries in July 1949.

Terms relating to the more elementary behaviour patterns such as reaction reflex, kineses, and taxis, have already been dealt with above so there remain the terms more specifically relating to the concept of instinct.

(a) INSTINCT: *an inherited and adapted system of co-ordination within the nervous system as a whole, which when activated finds expression in behaviour culminating in a fixed action pattern. It is organised on a hierarchical basis, both on the afferent and efferent sides. When 'charged', it shows evidence of action-specific potential and a readiness for release by an environmental releaser.*

(b) MOOD: this term was not at first included but was felt subsequently by a number of members to contain an idea essential to the concept of instinctive behaviour. The difficulty here was that the word had long been in use, on the one hand by human psychologists and by the general public to imply conscious subjective states, and on the other hand by some comparative ethologists specifically to exclude such states. Since the first use of the term had long priority it was difficult to dissociate psychological implications from it. Nevertheless its use in behaviour studies was not infrequent and it was found difficult to find a generally acceptable alternative. The following definition was therefore adopted.

MOOD: *the preliminary state of 'charge' or 'readiness for action' necessary to the performance of a given course of instinctive behaviour.*

(c) DRIVE: *the complex of internal and external states and stimuli leading to a given behaviour.* This is a wider definition than is sometimes employed; so that where the word is held to exclude the influence of external factors (as is often the case), it is perhaps best to use the qualifying adjective 'internal'. In its earliest usage in behaviour literature the term 'drive' implied little if anything more than a state of internal activity or dis-equilibrium either of the central nervous system or of glands which in turn stimulated the central nervous system. This activity could be conceived of as either actual or potential, for example some sort of state of tension or loading ready to activate the animal. This brings the term close to the usage of the word 'mood' (*Stimmung* in German).

(d) APPETITIVE BEHAVIOUR: *a variable introductory phase of an instinctive behaviour pattern or sequence.*

(e) CONSUMMATORY ACT: *an act which constitutes the termination of a given instinctive behaviour pattern or sequence.*

(f) FIXED ACTION PATTERN: *an inherited relatively complex movement pattern within instinctive behaviour, which is as characteristic of the species or group as are structural features.* (The intensity of its discharge may vary but its form is little, if at all, modifiable by external stimuli.)

(g) SPECIFIC ACTION POTENTIAL: *a state of the animal responsible for its readiness to perform the behaviour pattern of one instinct in preference to all other behaviour patterns.* (A specific readiness diminishes or disappears when the consummatory act of the charged instinct has been performed.)

(h) DISPLACEMENT ACTIVITY: *an activity resulting from the activation by the charge (specific action potential) of one or more instincts, of the action pattern belonging to another instinct. It seems to appear when a charged instinct is denied opportunity for adequate discharge through its own consummatory act or acts.* The term is not necessarily restricted to instinctive behaviour, and a much more general definition is often required—especially if applied to human behaviour. *An alternative version* to meet this need was provided by (i).

(i) DISPLACEMENT ACTIVITY: *the performance of a behaviour pattern out of the particular functional context of behaviour to which it is normally related.*

(j) RELEASER: *any specific feature or complex of features in a situation eliciting an instinctive activity or mood.*

(k) Sometimes during the period in question a distinction was made between releaser and social releaser. In this case we use SOCIAL RELEASER: *any specific feature or complex features of an organism eliciting an instinctive activity in another individual either of the same or another species.*

The 1949 Conference concluded with some definitions of terms used in the description and analysis of the learning process. While these are not here and now of particular importance it is perhaps useful for the sake of completeness to include the resulting definitions. Hence LEARNING: *the process which produces adaptive change in individual behaviour as a result of experience. It is regarded as distinct from fatigue, sensory adaptation, maturation and results of surgical or other injury.* HABITUATION: *the waning of a response as a result of repeated stimulation which is not followed by any kind of reinforcement. It is of relatively enduring nature and is thus regarded as distinct from fatigue and sensory adaptation.* REINFORCE-MENT: *any object, situation, or activity which leads to a more stable or complete state of the organism by the acquisition or conservation of reserves, release of a consummatory act, or the fuller organisation of sense data (perception of external stimuli).* If this use of the term reinforcement is adopted, 'reward' then becomes positive reinforcement and 'punishment' negative reinforcement.

As to the general topic of conditioning, it was realised then, as is still true now, that there were a very large number of synonyms for the classical conditioned reflex. For the general purposes of the behaviour student the following definition of conditioning was reached. CONDITIONING: *the process of acquisition by an animal of the capacity to respond to a given stimulus with a reflex action proper to another stimulus (reinforcement) when the two stimuli are applied concurrently for a number of times.* TRIAL AND ERROR LEARNING: *the development of an association, as the result of reinforcement during appetitive behaviour, between a stimulus or situation and an independent motor action as an item in that behaviour when both stimulus and motor action precede the reinforcement in time and the motor action is not the inevitable inherited response to the reinforcement.* It was pointed out that one unsatisfactory aspect of the term 'trial and error' is that there is no convenient name in English for behaviour acquired by this process. We are thus reduced to calling such behaviour 'habit' or 'habit-forming', a term which has a much wider meaning and is usually applied to well-established behaviour, whatever type of learning has been involved. LATENT LEARNING: *the association of indifferent stimuli or situations without patent reinforcement.* It was pointed out that latent learning involves delayed response and transfer of training and is particularly characteristic of animals which tend to explore their environment without the satisfaction of any immediate reward, but by their exploration securing information which may afterwards be of use to them in a number of contexts, for example in food getting, in escape, or in finding their way home to nest or territory. This amounts to saying that much latent learning is really exploratory learning, a term which has come into great favour recently. IMPRINTING: *a rapid and usually very stable form of learning taking place in the early life of social species, whereby, and apparently without any need of 'reinforcement', broad supra-individual charac-*

*teristics of the species come to be recognised as a 'species-pattern' and
subsequently used as releasers.*

Lorenz's formulation of his system of instinctive behaviour, if
looked at anew today, may strike many workers as in so many
respects naive and problematical, that they fail to realise the
immense significance it held for the naturalists, physiologists, and
ethologists of the time. To the workers of those days, the first and
obvious advantage was that it offered a co-ordinated system which
at once suggested where new observations and experiments, and
new ideas, could be directed so as to be most fruitful. Some of his
models were obviously analogous only—but the very essence of
'analogy' is its imperfection which challenges rethinking. One did
not suppose them to be 'true' but they were valuable in being
highly suggestive. Conversely a model which is too good and too
close may be, for that very reason, infertile.[3] Thus Lorenz's
scheme invited, and made enormously easier, the causal analysis
of behaviour. Secondly it did not eliminate the psychological
approach but made clear where, in those days, it was most useful
and essential (as in the purposive highly plastic phases of the
appetitive behaviour and releaser behaviour) and where for the
time being at least it was relatively useless—within the confines of
the instinctive act in the strict usage. Thirdly Lorenz's concept of
instinct explained the great contradiction which was manifest in so
much previous work on animal intelligence. Again and again we
were reminded how past workers would disagree as to the 'intelligence' or 'stupidity' of a particular animal. This for the first time
became more easily understandable. When an elaborate instinct
goes off in the biologically right circumstances the whole behaviour
appeared wonderfully purposive; and if the investigator happened
to be studying the modifiable aspects of one of the higher examples
of appetitive behaviour, where learning plays an important part,
he might rightly conclude that the animal was 'intelligent'. On
the other hand if the experimenter, when studying the hard core
of instinct (which was regarded by Lorenz as essentially fixed),
could by his experimental method manoeuvre an animal into an
unfamiliar situation, so that a stereotyped instinct found expression
in the wrong circumstances, the same animal would of course ap-

pear very stupid. An obvious example of this is the already known fact that a jackdaw (*Corvus monedula*) cannot recognise its own eggs however strikingly marked they may be, and many birds will accept quite absurd objects for incubation as egg substitutes. Yet, as Lorenz long before had shown, a jackdaw can very quickly learn to know individual human beings and also to recognise twenty or more individual jackdaws which make up his flock. Again it was already known that many birds may be extremely good at learning landmarks and the details of their territory but extremely 'stupid' in dealing with any untoward incidents in nesting or rearing their young—aspects of behaviour which are normally governed to a very high degree by instinct. Finally, this scheme of Lorenz explained very conveniently a whole series of otherwise puzzling and awkward facts grouped under the headings of 'displacement reactions'. It was soon seen that displacement activities tended to be elicited in three types of situation. (a) When two antagonistic drives were simultaneously aroused, for instance in defence or the urge to brood and the urge to retreat. (b) When the goal of a drive was reached so expeditiously as to leave a surplus of aroused 'energy'—as when an adversary suddenly disappeared, or coition is suddenly consummated. Again, it soon became clear that displacement appears when an external stimulus link is missing in a chain sequence of interaction; as when, after courtship preliminaries in birds, coition is not accomplished and completely irrelevant movements appear. This has been shown particularly by Kortlandt (1940) as a result of his study of the cormorant (*Phalacrocorax carbo*).[4] He found that when an aroused impulse is denied an expression it, as he said, 'sparks over' to a definite behaviour group, usually the same no matter what the nature of the thwarting cause. And it was soon shown that such displacements could have an important secondary function by serving as a social signal for releasing special responses in other individuals of the same species. That is to say they tend to be ritualized and play a very important part in social organisation as social releasers.

In short, Lorenz's formulation gave an enormous stimulus, firstly to those who had been keeping inventories or ethograms of behaviour as a complete inventory of the behaviour of an animal in the field or in the wild, enumerating what its various responses or reactions were and where they fitted into its normal life cycle and experience. His system also made laboratory experiments on behaviour enormously more rewarding; by such experiments one could, among many other things, identify and itemize particular circumstances which allowed the given behaviour to proceed— either by supplying a releaser, or by concentrating the animal's attention on other parts of the environment at a particular time. Out of this arose the 'isolation experiment' in which an animal was reared from the egg, or the earliest active stage, out of contact with its own species. By doing this it became apparent that when the elaborate actions appeared they were in some way programmed internally (either in the central nervous system or by the neuro-muscular structure, and co-ordination of the whole animal) and were in this sense innate. In addition Lorenz's system offered an enormous stimulus to the neurophysiologist and the neuro-anatomist. For it specified points in the sequences of behaviour at which the drive might best be analysed and in what sense the term 'endogenous' might reasonably be used.

Similarly it gave an equally strong incentive to the study of endocrine organs, of endocrinology and ultimately of the place in action of hormones within the animal organism. Once again in relation to the development of releasers, the study of the sense organs of animals became of enormously greater importance and interest. In particular it became urgently desirable to know whether a given circumstance acted as a releaser because the limitations of the sense organs caused the animal to respond to only a limited part of the total environmental situation, or whether, alternatively, the animal was constructing its own sensory field by means of some sort of *gestalt* development and recognition. Finally, the Lorenzian system provided an enormous stimulus for the study of genetics in relation to animal behaviour. For one must emphasize once again the fact that behavioural characteristics were often found to be so constant and predictable that they are capable of serving as specific characters in just the same way and often to the same degree as are bodily structures.

Perhaps we can sum up the whole matter by giving a provisional restatement of the position of Lorenz's theory of instinctive behaviour, in about 1947. We may say that instinct is a specific stereotyped inherited pattern of behaviour, an inborn movement form, often incorporating systems of chain-reflexes, but governed and co-ordinated by a combination of central nervous system activity and *proprioceptive* stimuli. Thus *instinct*, in the strict sense, forms the *drive* by building up an *internal tension* of *reaction-specific energy* in the central nervous system, often associated with a particular *physiological need* or *mental state*. The drive was seen as giving rise to the *appetitive behaviour* with its associated *taxes* and *kineses* which lead the animal to the *goal* situation where the instinctive act finds its natural *releaser*. This releaser is often a complex environmental pattern. It was thought to act *via* a *receptory correlate* in the higher centres of the central nervous system, a correlate which fits the releaser as a lock fits the key. This *receptory correlate*, which often involves recognition of an elaborate visual pattern—a complex *gestalt*—had, in the then existing state of physiological knowledge, to be conceived solely in psychological terms. If the animal is prevented from reaching the goal situation the Lorenzian assumption was that the reaction-specific energy continues to accumulate, increasing the internal tension, so that *lowering of the threshold* and perhaps *vacuum activity* (*leerlauf*) would be observed. This vacuum activity or *leerlauf* was regarded as the instinctive act being forced out by its own internal tension without the intervention of a releaser or other external stimulus at all. It was also stressed, however, that the so-called reaction-specific energy was not always as reaction-specific as Lorenz had first thought; but might, if one outlet is dammed up, flow off into another according to a definite *hierarchy* of *displacement reactions*. Instinct was regarded as capable of being finely adjusted to the exact details of the environment by what von Holst called the 'coat of reflexes' governed by exteroceptive stimuli. In so far as proprioceptive reflexes played a part in co-ordination and in so far as these were modifiable there would then be scope for improvement with practice and acquirement of skill. Conditioning of the exteroceptive reflexes would also of course contribute to this. Finally it was shown[5] that an instinctive act may not always be a conspicuous form of behaviour but may include such behaviour as sleep or resting where the situation sought is one of minimal stimulation. So the core of *instinctive behaviour* in the wide sense was thought to be the instinctive movement (in the strict sense) basically stereotyped, rigid, and difficult, if not impossible, of modification. Instinctive behaviour in the wide sense also included drive, appetitive behaviour, and goal behaviour. And in the last two particularly, the whole field of animal learning was raised by the possibility, now realised, of modification by reflex conditioning, by trial-and-error learning, by observational learning, by latent learning, and by insight and insight learning. So here again new fields of great promise and interest were in due course open to the learning theorist and the experimenter.

REFERENCES

1. Muller, G. E., *Abriss der Psychologie* (Gottingen, 1924).
2. For an admirable summary of Lorenz's overall position see Tinbergen, N., 'An objective study of the innate behaviour of animals', *Biblioteca Biotheoretica*, 1942, **1**, 40–98.
3. Hinde, R. A., *Brit. J. Philos. Sci.*, 1956, **6**, 321–31.
4. Kortland, A., 'Eine Ubersicht der angeborenen Verhaltenweisen des Mitteleuropäischen Kormorans (*Phalocrocorax carbo Sinensis*)', *Arch. heerl. Zool.*, 1940, **14**, 401–42.
5. Holzapfel, M., *Naturwiss.*, 1940, **28**, 273–80.

7

New post-war research groups and laboratories

When the war in Europe ended, the recommencement of ethological studies on the continent was—bearing in mind the shattering dislocation, physical, psychological, and social—wonderfully rapid. We will attempt to outline this remarkable regrowth briefly, considering it principally as a response to the eight papers of Konrad Lorenz.

The end of the war reached Austria before other parts of Europe and hence the resumption of animal behaviour studies commenced, as was not surprising, in Vienna. The first steps were taken at a time when Lorenz was still in captivity in Russia and rumours that he was dead were being circulated. The moving spirits at this period in Vienna were Otto König and his wife Lili. During the war years König was on active service with the Austrian Army in southern Italy. He kept in contact with Lili in Vienna by frequent illustrated letters describing the charms of nature and natural history of the island of Sicily—so transparently simple and genuine that they escaped the attentions of military censorship. These letters were published as a small book and were a great success in Vienna: a refreshing relief from the horrors and anxieties of war. The Königs had little or no money except what they received from this book, but this was indeed a windfall; and with characteristic enthusiasm and confidence they risked everything in founding a small institute, 'Biologische Station Wilhelminenberg', for the study of animal behaviour. They immediately started 'squatting', together with half-a-dozen students of biology from Vienna University, on an area of land on the outskirts of

Vienna, formerly the property of an Austrian Archduke, which was the site of a German anti-aircraft battery. Fortunately their 'squat' was not contested and they immediately took over the abandoned battery and with their own hands transformed huts, earthworks, and site into everything they needed—living accommodation, aviaries, aquaria, laboratories, etc. Otto König had been a pupil of Lorenz, who at the end of 1947 returned, as from the dead, to his old home at Altenberg (Greifenstein) to find an embryonic but prospering little institute only a few miles away.

The primary programme of the Biologische Station Wilhelminenberg consisted mainly of the production of complete ethograms of key species very much in the Lorenzian manner. Otto König resumed his earlier work on the bearded tit (*Panurus biarmicus russicus*) in the swamps of the Neusiedler See—a reserve of great richness which has been perhaps the chief field area of the institute throughout its thirty-two years of life. This and other species of birds were with great skill reared from the egg in aviaries, and were bred in captivity, so an immense amount of new information was obtained. Besides this, an extensive comparative study of five species of herons and also of several members of the family *Rallidae* was undertaken. For a long time the station was severely handicapped by shortage of funds; and the work on the rails, birds which are extremely expensive to maintain, had to be cut short for this reason. Another line of work was a very promising study of the behavioural repertoire of the bee-eater (*Merops apiaster*) which was also successfully reared from the egg and from the early nestling stage. The study of the genesis of the behaviour which involved catching and killing the prey was particularly rewarding. As well as these bird studies, the station in its early years managed to carry out work on mammals, reptiles, and amphibia, the latter including a fine investigation by Eibl-Eibesfeldt on the toad (*Bufo bufo*).[1]

In its early years the station ran a popular and beautifully illustrated journal entitled *Umwelt* and this initiated what was to prove a steadily increasing programme of educational work. Support was eventually forthcoming on a small scale from the

Vienna Academy of Sciences; but, partly as a result of the financial stringency, the station launched out into the production of nature instructional films, initially for sale and later for television, many of which are of the highest quality. Thus the Wilhelminenberg made a substantial contribution to the post-war development of ethology, particularly in central Europe.

A figure of immense importance in the immediate post-war development of ethology was Erich von Holst. As we have seen, the instinct theories of Konrad Lorenz laid great stress on the scientific and objective investigation of the drive behind fixed action patterns, on the co-ordination of these patterns with each other, and the momentous question of the origin of the drive in the central nervous system. Until the mid 1930s the vast majority of neuro-physiological studies of behaviour were concerned with the nature and co-ordination of reflex action and any effective neuro-physiological theory of 'instinct' was conspicuously absent. Von Holst's main interest was *behavioural physiology* and since he was in the milieu created mainly by the work of Heinroth, von Uexküll, and Lorenz, he was very much alive to the implications of the kinds of behaviour which they were describing and investigating. In fact their studies acted as a focal point for many of the developments in ethology.

As has already been stressed, ethologists are concerned with observing the behaviour of intact animals, with the minimum of interference and under conditions which as closely as possible approach those of the natural habitat. As a neuro-physiologist von Holst's approach was of course different in that he employed active intervention in the central nervous system as a means of understanding more about its function in controlling the behaviour of the whole animal. So it was inevitable that he would become particularly interested in the *spontaneous* action of the central nervous system in addition to the aspect previously so widely studied: the relationship between stimulus and response. He was able to demonstrate that the central system does not passively link stimuli to responses but is highly active in itself, producing 'internal stimuli' and incorporating numerous functional systems. As Robert Martin, the translator of recently published volumes of the selected papers of von Holst, points out, von Holst demonstrated beyond doubt that it is not merely the structure of the brain and its accessory systems which is inherited, but also an entire range of spontaneously active mechanisms which are indispensable to the performance of species—characteristic patterns of behaviour. A very common early criticism of the Lorenzian theory of instinct was that it made totally unacceptable, indeed impossible, demands upon the central nervous system—demands which no reputable neurophysiologist would believe the structure capable of fulfilling. Von Holst showed that there were a large number of mechanisms within the nervous system, the function of which was yet little understood. But he was confident that the whole central nervous system was an hierarchical system, with many different functional parts. He says, in 'Relations between the Central Nervous System and the Peripheral Organs',[2] 'we recognise fragments of mechanisms and some of them we call "reflexes"; this term denotes fragments of very different mechanisms.' Thus he had demonstrated that the central nervous system is not 'a passive system linking stimuli to the responses, it is a highly active organ continually producing its own stimuli'. It is extraordinary today to realise how heretical such a conclusion (which was in fact by no means entirely new) seemed to many neurophysiologists of the time.

Von Holst's first major paper appeared in 1935 when he was a professor at Heidelberg and all his output was encompassed between that date and his tragically early death in 1962. He was able to resume scientific work after the war in 1948 through the assistance of the Max-Planck Gesellschaft which provided accommodation in temporary and highly inadequate quarters in an uncompleted naval barracks at Wilhelmshaven. Here, with his two brilliant pupils, Bernard Hassenstein and Horst Mittelstaedt, he inaugurated a research centre of exceptional promise. A full Planck Professorship was established in 1954 and the Max-Planck Institute for Behavioural Physiology was inaugurated in 1958 at Seewissen-bei-Starnberg, in Bavaria—Erich von Holst was the Director and Konrad Lorenz his close collaborator. The name of the Institute itself reflects the importance of von Holst's approach to the behaviour of whole animals and is a memorial to his immense influence on the development of ethology.

Similarly, Konrad Lorenz, who on his return from captivity had (for some years) only his own home at Altenberg in which to carry on his work, was later given full support by the Max-Planck Society and was provided in 1950 with excellent facilities at Buldern in Westphalia. His unit was transferred from there to Seewiesen in 1958.

Ethology received another early accession of strength from Otto Köhler, Professor of Zoology at Freiburg im Briesgau, who,

Figure 12 Professor Otto Köhler. Photograph taken in Freiburg, 1957.

together with Lorenz, was a founder editor of *Zeitschrift für Tierpsychologie* in 1937. Although Köhler's early behavioural work was primarily concerned with taxes and kinesis, he was an immediate convert to the new ideas about instinct. He did not himself do much to develop these, but he made a really great contribution to the study of animal behaviour by his investigation of the number sense or 'counting ability' of animals. Previously there had been attempts for the best part of a hundred years to show that animals were able to count, but there was always some deficiency in the experimental procedure, some loophole left unclosed which rendered the results suspect. It was the outstanding feat of Otto Köhler and his pupils to produce the final but absolutely unequivocal results which showed that animals, especially birds, can 'think un-named numbers'—that is, they have a pre-linguistic number sense; to some extent, they think without words. This is an achievement with which Otto Köhler's name will always be linked.

Of course during the whole period in question, the continuing incomparable work of Karl von Frisch was having a growing influence on ethology. This led to his sharing the Nobel Prize with Lorenz and Tinbergen in 1973. He never, I believe, used the term 'ethology' in his writings, and as he has been fully discussed in Chapter 5 above, as far senior to Lorenz, little more need be said here. Suffice it to point out that while he has throughout had the same basic naturalist's approach, it led him first into sensory physiology and only later did his studies on the sensory physiology of the honey-bee lead him to what may be described as a full 'ethogram' of the worker bee. This raised many of the most crucial theoretical problems with which ethologists and psychologists are concerned.[3]

It is difficult to know where to start the account of Holland, a country whose pioneering efforts in ethology were so important and so numerous. It is probably best to commence with the completely new developments in the University of Groningen.

Gerard Baerends, in his earlier years at Leiden University, distinguished himself in two fields, fish biology and ecology and a magnificent study, begun at Hulshorst with Niko Tinbergen's team, on the reproductive behaviour and ability in orientation of the digger wasp (*Ammophila campestris*). This was published in full in 1941 and was a very model of ethological investigations in that it raised all the problems of the nature of instinct, of appetitive behaviour, and of releasers; at the same time linking them with overwhelming evidence of the extraordinarily elaborate releaser system and the almost unbelievable subtlety and precision of memory and of orientation by means of landmarks. He showed that the wasp was able to keep 'in mind' a whole series of nests in different states of provisioning, make visits of inspection, and, as a result of what was perceived on these visits, carry out the appropriate actions ensuring the full development of the offspring. Baerends had also done extensive work as a fishery officer on the ecology and behaviour of fish.

In 1946 Baerends was appointed Professor of Zoology in the University of Groningen and immediately elaborated a far-reaching programme of ethology with ecology; so that the laboratory was primarily if not entirely concerned with the activity of 'the animal as a whole'. From the educational point of view he arranged things so that the whole field of zoology could be covered in the lectures, but as to research, nearly all the staff were concerned with developing ethological studies on the broadest possible basis. In the early years at Groningen, Baerends himself concentrated on the releasers for egg-recognition in gulls and the factors controlling incubation behaviour. His work on egg-recognition started with the concept of the innate releasive mechanism in mind. But during the course of years it became clear that in order to understand the results properly, a more subtle system of interacting motivational systems, particularly the hierarchy concept, was necessary.

Although the emphasis of the Department was emphatically on the activity of the animal as a whole, it was not long before a study of the neurophysiological mechanisms underlying behaviour was undertaken. This led eventually to the application of techniques such as brain lesioning, brain stimulation, self-stimulation in a Skinner box, measuring action potentials of various parts of the brain, and sophisticated assessments of the levels of glucose, fatty acids, and insulin in the blood. So the way was open for endocrino-logical studies. Nor were birds neglected. Here again the motive was the study of the ontogeny of complex behaviour in close con-nexion with comparative studies on displays. The *Phasianidae*, with their magnificent and elaborate display systems, were chosen for this work and after a preliminary study the decision was made to concentrate on the red jungle fowl (*Gallus gallus*), the supposed ancestor of all forms of the domestic fowl.

What has been described by no means exhausts the full range and complexity of the work so successfully commenced at Groningen. But it can be said without hesitation that in a very few years the zoology department equipped itself for active research in almost all the main problems and opportunities posed by the Lorenzian system; and probably by the early 1950s the teaching of ethology and related fields at Groningen was far in advance of that obtainable at any other university. By the end of the 1950s there were twenty staff members of which fifteen were primarily interested in research and teaching in one or other aspects of ethology.

We come now to the key personality in the Dutch scene, Niko Tinbergen. Niko had been appointed Assistant in the Leiden Department of Zoology (at a salary of about £150 per annum!) in 1931. His early development has been discussed in a preceding part of this book and after the interruption of the war he was able to resume his work at Leiden and prosecute further (by means of Field Assistantships and D.Phil studies) the very successful methods of teaching which he had previously evolved. Niko tells me that the total budget for the field work was still very small indeed. For a tent and some aquaria the student had to apply for special grants, each one of approximately £25 altogether. Travel, up to seventy miles, had to be mainly on a bicycle and all campers in Hulshorst had to have their own little tent and paid 6d a week towards a saucepan fund, etc. It is refreshing to consider how, in many fields, work of the most profound significance can be accomplished with almost derisory financial support.

In 1949 Tinbergen, happy and successful though he was at Leiden, was finding the administrative and other duties of a

Figure 13 Niko Tinbergen, photographed in Cambridge, 1959.

professor increasingly onerous. Therefore when he was offered the post of Lecturer in Zoology at Oxford by Sir Alister Hardy with the aim of developing an animal behaviour research group there, he felt bound to accept. I feel little doubt that this acceptance was in part an expression of his deep concern to develop and intensify international contacts in science and to help make sure that ethology was not considered the peculiar province of middle Europe. Moerover he believed that Britain, with its strong natural history tradition, could be an admirable milieu for the development of ethology. (He did not know at that time that an ethological group was just starting up in Cambridge.) Niko rightly points out that until then naturalists in Britain who were potential ethologists tended to become ecologists, and those in the USA behaviourists; a situation which was far from satisfactory or even reasonable. He was also taking into account in this country the early work of Selous, Huxley, Howard, and others with the strongly developing Association for the Study of Animal Behaviour

To start with the financial conditions in Oxford were little if at all an improvement on those he had experienced in Holland. His initial salary in Oxford was hardly appropriate for the rearing of a large family, but in spite of this he felt that Oxford seemed a good place to go, and he had few if any qualms about leaving Holland for he knew that ethology was safe in the hands of Gerard Baerends and his successor in Leiden, Jan van Iersel. Later results certainly confirmed his confidence about this. Tinbergen fully agreed with Sir Alister Hardy that he should not attempt to organise a separate sub-department, but should be just a group in the Department of Zoology. Hardy obtained a grant of £500 for him for one year from the Agricultural Research Council and then a five-year grant from the Nuffield Foundation: £10 000 over five years, which was as Niko says quite considerable for such a small group working in such an obscure field! The main reason why these exiguous grants (which were tiny compared with those given in other fields to other centres) were satisfactory was that repeated discussions and re-assessment of the idea that a separate group divorced from the the Zoology laboratory was rejected by all parties. Niko tells me that, all in all, he was convinced that the decision to remain a small group in the corner of the Department of Zoology was a wise one; if only because he knew from experience in Leiden that he would have been a bad Head of Department!

During the previous ten to twenty years in Holland Niko could never discern a clear directional line in the activities of his pupils. The same situation obtained for a while in Oxford; the work there included, among other things, an evolutionary approach to signals and their ritualization, of which continuation of the gull studies was an essential part. But over the years the original piecemeal approach of Niko's book *The Study of Instinct* and the variety in thesis subjects and quality of theses, began to show a gradually acquired direction. Niko's own work and that of the pupils nearest to him became part of 'behavioural ecology' and he feels that this can be said to characterize the best of what was typical of his group much later. As will be evident later in this book, this field was greatly enlarged to include some neurophysiology, the study of behavioural development in young birds, the 'searching image' and related problems, and genetics and behaviour in *Drosophila*. Incidentally, in evaluating the Oxford experience and his work there over a long period of years, Niko tells me that he considers it a serious fault in the British system that a Ph.D. may be awarded before any of the work has been published. In this country we sometimes think that the continental system of insisting that treatises are with the printer, or in printed form, results in publication of immature and poorly considered work. Niko points out that the continental system gives the supervisor the authority to insist upon the publication of good work, whereas here he may exert his utmost pressure on the young doctor but has no power.

As with Leiden, the establishment of ethology in Cambridge had a long 'pre-history' of which I am part. As an insect physiologist with a particular interest in respiratory problems, I had become involved in the study of respiratory adaptations of the larvae of parasitoids in their insect hosts. This led me to an interest in host-selection by the adult and so to the study of olfaction and olfactory responses, since these are the prime methods by which the host is recognised by an adult female when she is ready to oviposit. This study commenced in 1936 and the first paper on the modification of the olfactory recognition of the host through experience was published in 1937. The problem was to explain the complete host-specificity of some forms of some species, and the ability to develop strains of the species concerned attached to particular hosts—whether to the plant on which the hosts feed or to the insect hosts themselves. During a laboratory study of such responses I and some of my colleagues were investigating the tendency, which seemed quite evident, of some parasitic insects to confine their egg laying to the species of hosts on which they themselves had been reared. This was investigated and described as 'olfactory conditioning'. And for a while the term 'conditioning' seemed adequate to describe and label what was taking place. But then I obtained some clear examples, with the parasitic Hymen-

Figure 14 The author, W. H. Thorpe, in 1959.

opteroid *Nemeritis canescens*, of the host-search and oviposition responses of the adult insect being significantly affected by the particular species of host from which it had itself emerged. This was indeed a surprise since it revealed learned behaviour of a complexity and precision far exceeding the correct use of the term 'conditioning' and in fact involving what the comparative psychologists in the USA were already calling 'latent learning' and even 'insight learning'—a behaviour which ethologists were describing as 'imprinting'.

Thus it was that I came to read the five great papers of Konrad Lorenz referred to above (page 67) and realised for the first time where my studies were leading me—straight into the ethological field. I concluded that what I was really primarily interested in as an entomologist and insect physiologist was the relationship between instinct in the ethologist's sense and learning in the sense of the American psychologists. I had been a keen field ornithologist

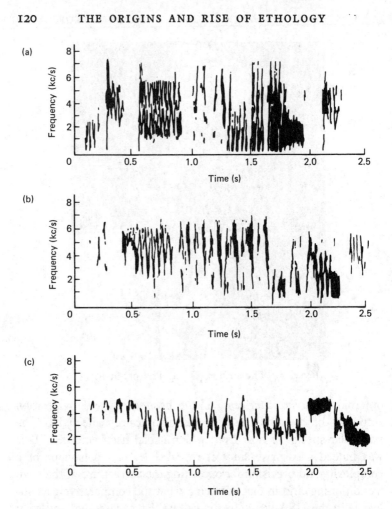

Figure 15 Three stages in the sub-song of the chaffinch.
(a) Chirps and rattles having a large range of frequencies.
(b) Transition to full song. (c) Spring song.

for many years and it struck me very forcibly that for the particular work I hoped to do, birds would provide the most promising material. The reasons for this conclusion were quite simple: birds provided on the one hand some of the most striking examples of elaborate instinctive behaviour (as in their display, feeding methods, nest building, etc.), and at the same time they were

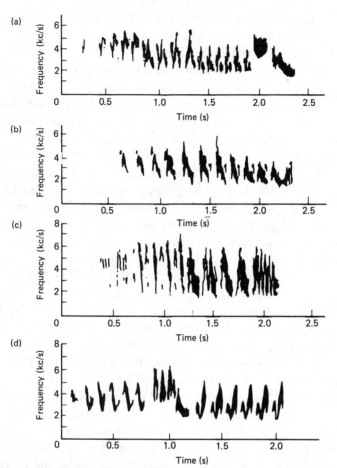

Figure 16 Song of chaffinch (*Fringilla coelebs*) showing its modification in development through experience. (After Thorpe, 1961.) (a) normal song; (b) an individual reared in isolation; (c) an individual from a group reared in isolation; (d) an individual reared in isolation, after tutoring with a rearticulated chaffinch song with the ending in the middle.

capable of extraordinary feats of learning (as in their migratory and homing orientation), and, in the song birds especially, of imitative learning of a high order. So I decided that at all costs I must attempt to switch over from entomology to ornithology.

By the greatest good fortune and with the keen assistance of the then Professor of Zoology, Sir James Gray, my proposal to establish an ornithological field station where birds could be reared in aviaries and pens and their behaviour studied both in captivity and in the wild was enthusiastically received. By 1943 I had already commenced some bird studies, strictly limited though they were by the facilities of a 'down town' zoological laboratory. But by 1950 the University had secured for me a four-acre site at Madingley for what was then called an 'ornithological field station'. Thus in 1949, as Niko Tinbergen was preparing to leave Leiden for Oxford, I was preparing to transfer my research from the main zoological department in Cambridge to Madingley.

Our primary objectives in the first years of Madingley were firstly, general comparative studies on the display and other species-specific behaviour of a number of species and genera of finches. Secondly, intensive studies on the following responses and resulting imprinting were undertaken with the moorhen (*Gallinula chloropus*), domestic chick, and duckling. Thirdly, studies of song and song-learning, which had already begun, primarily with the chaffinch (*Fringilla coelebs*), were intensified. This work on the specificity of vocal repertoire and the means of its individual elaboration proved particularly rewarding; owing to the fortunate chance of the rapid development of recording techniques, first on disc and then on tape, and above all by the sound spectrograph, which made it possible for the first time to carry out precise analyses of individual consistency and variation in bird voices and the contribution of innate factors, early experience, and imitative abilities to the development of these voices. Indeed it is not too much to say that the study of bird vocalizations would have been completely impossible without the new recording methods and very greatly handicapped, to the point of total failure, without the invention of the sound spectrograph.

With the institution of a separate field station decided upon, the problem of its day-to-day direction and curatorship arose. Since I already had a considerable teaching load as a University Lecturer coupled with heavy responsibilities as a College Fellow and Tutor, it was impossible for me to undertake these duties also.

At that time I became fully aware of the great difficulties, financial and otherwise, facing Konrad Lorenz in Vienna. So I suggested to James Gray that if we were able to lure Konrad over to be the resident superintendent, the venture would get off to a splendid start. Gray agreed; and I wrote to Konrad inviting him to come, in spite of the fact that the salary we had to offer was minimal. Konrad replied immediately that he would come and quoted P. G. Wodehouse to the effect that he was 'prepared to start at the bottom of the ladder and work his way steadily downwards'! However almost immediately the Max-Planck Gesellschaft made a most impressive offer to Konrad of an institute of his own in Germany—and my dream of a resounding and dramatic inauguration of a British programme of ethology suffered an abrupt awakening! It is intriguing now to speculate what the ultimate effect on ethology in this country (and not only here) might have been.

Fortunately a most promising alternative to Lorenz was possible: Robert A. Hinde was appointed Curator in Charge of the Madingley Field Station with a minute 'office' in the disused blacksmith's shop at Madingley, and a full-time aviary keeper was secured. Among our first intake of students were G. V. T. Matthews (who made orientation studies in gulls, on the Manx shearwater (*Puffinus puffinus*), and on homing pigeons) and Peter Marler (who commenced his studies on the aggressive displays of the chaffinch, as examples of appetitive and consummatory behaviour and from this developed his investigations into the song and the significance of its individual variation). In addition to these Hinde carried out a critical study of the nature of the visual stimulus which the form and facial disc of owls present and which leads to the 'mobbing response' of so many small birds. This included a detailed study of the bird's habituation to such models and the various circumstances which govern the rate and degree of decrement of the response over lengthy periods. At the same time I was carrying out studies on imprinting and the following response of a number of species of precocial birds.

Some reference at this stage should be made to the quick involvement in ethology of zoological gardens in Europe (a tradition inaugurated thirty years before by Zuckerman at the London Zoological Gardens and by Heinroth in Germany). Firstly the work at Basle under H. Hediger must be mentioned; especially the studies of his pupil, R. Schenkel on wolves. Similarly at Berne early results consisted of a paper by H. R. Räber on the display behaviour of the turkey (*Meleagris*) and on the owls, *Asio* and *Strix*.

The renaissance of ethology in France was initiated by the great biologist and scholar Pierre-Paul Grassé. A full bibliography of his works is provided as an appendix to his scientific jubilee volume *Pages Choisies* (Paris: Masson & Cie, 1967). More recently two ethological stations, of great promise and independent outlook, have emerged; the first under Remy Chauvin at the Sorbonne in Paris and the second headed by Gaston Richard at Rennes. The Paris group has produced a series of valuable papers by Darchen on the behaviour of various Insecta and Arachnida. Chauvin himself is the author of comprehensive works on the honey bee and other Hymenoptera. There is also a recent outstanding study by Chauvin-Muckensturm.[4] This shows that great spotted woodpeckers (*Dendrocopus major*) can learn a simple telegraphic drumming code by which they request whichever of five types of food they wish to obtain from the experimenter at a particular time. When a woodpecker had learned to use this drumming code to communicate with the experimenter, other persons with whom the bird was not familiar were also able to communicate, with approximately equal effectiveness.

Finally, the situation in the USA must be mentioned. The vast majority of American workers on behaviour were of course comparative psychologists of the behaviourist approach who were not likely to be particularly responsive to the new ideas about instinct. It is true that Lashley, who as we have seen arrived independently at all the essential ideas of Lorenz, was still active at Orange Park, but he was fully occupied with his intelligence and neurophysiological studies on chimpanzees. However, there were two notable exceptions. C. R. Carpenter, of State College, Pennsylvania, wrote splendid papers resulting from field observation of howler monkeys (*Alouatta palliata*) and of gibbons (*Hylo-*

bates), and F. A. Beach, Professor of Psychology at Yale University, was the world authority on the effect of hormones on the sexual behaviour of mammals. His ready acceptance of the coming of ethology had far-reaching effects on the spread and development of ethology in the United States. Both joined the editorial staff of *Behaviour* at its commencement in 1948—as did Hediger and Köhler. So also did T. C. Schneirla, of the American Museum of Natural History, who was famed for his studies on the biology of army ants and was initially a strong opponent of Lorenzian ideas. But he slowly came round, largely through the influence of D. Lehrman, to a reconsideration of the basic questions raised by ethology, and during the years 1956–66 produced valuable critical and closely reasoned papers.

REFERENCES

1. Eibl-Eibesfeldt, I., *Zeit. Tierpsychologie*, 1951, **8**, 370–400; *Behaviour*, 1951, **4**, 1–35.
2. von Holst, E., *British J. Animal Behav.*, 1954, **2**, 89–94.
3. Griffin, D. R., *The Question of Animal Awareness* (New York: Rocke-feller University Press, 1976).
4. Chauvin-Muckensturm, B., *Rev. comp. Animal*, 1974, **9**, 185–207.

8

The present position of ethological concepts and research

It is obvious that the explosive development of ethological research in the last twenty-five years has produced a total mass of information the fully adequate summary of which would require at least a large volume and certainly a group of collaborators, rather than a single author. So to attempt any full and detailed conspectus in a single chapter of a small book such as this is unthinkable. But it does, at least, seem worthwhile attempting to indicate present trends—though in doing so the treatment must inevitably become more physiological and hence more technical, than in previous chapters.

Such a survey of trends will, it is hoped, show where the original concepts of classical ethology (as outlined in Chapter 6) have led us, and what value they may still have for further development. Furthermore, it should yield a very general idea of the present position of the subject—or rather many subjects—now comprised in the overall term 'ethology'; and give us some clues as to what the future may hold for the discipline.

Fixity of behaviour patterns

It seems appropriate to start with a concept which was in many ways central to the classical ethology, namely that of *fixed action patterns*. This concept was one of the most precisely defined and observationally striking in the early days of ethology. I think it can be stated without serious questioning that it has stood up to examination remarkably well and shows no real signs of diminished usefulness. It was only to be expected that the adjective 'fixed' is less rigidly employed now than it was. Although the fixity of, for instance, the cocoon-constructing movements which an insect larva employs, the extraordinary signal movements by which each species of fiddler crab (*Uca*) reveals its specific identity, or the display of a peacock, are eye-catching even to an inexperienced observer; close and extensive observation is likely to reveal more variety than was at one time supposed. Nevertheless, fixity of these actions is indeed in many cases phenomenal. For it has been one of the achievements of ethology to show that such actions are very often as reliable for systematic distinction and classification of species as are any structural features traditionally used for such purposes. In other words, they are as much part of the order of construction of the species as are the genitalia of a *Lepidopteron*, the number of hairs on the thorax of a *Dipteron*, or the feather structure and formula of a bird's wing. Real advance in the understanding of fixed action patterns has been shown in the development of our views as to the importance of the intensity of the action, and the realisation that (a) the perfect control of intensity, (b) the timing, and (c) the speed of the fixed action pattern may be as important as, and often more important than, the rigidity and precision with which the action is normally performed.

As one example of extreme rigidity which can be found in bird displays (and one where intensity differences are almost absent)

Table 1. *Well-established and stereotyped behaviour patterns (Table 2 from Fentress, 1976).*

---

1. Demand less processing capacity for performance
2. Relatively independent from sensory guidance (i.e., centrally controlled)
3. Often appear when processing capacity reduced or approaching limit, and/or when sources of sensory modulation reduced
4. Provide convenient 'simplified' model system for study of behavioural integration
5. Emphasize importance of capacity limitations and phenotypic structure in studies of integrated behaviour

---

we may cite the duration of the 'head-throw' display of the golden-eye duck (*Bucephala clangula*). This has a mean duration of 1.29 seconds and a standard deviation of only ±0.08 seconds. Hinde[1] points out that such exceptional constancy is especially characteristic of the signal movements used in intraspecific communication. Fentress[2] argues that when the processing demands of the organism begin to outstrip the organism's processing capacities there is an increased probability that (a) ongoing sequences of behaviour will become more stereotyped, tightly organized, less flexible, and more autonomous, and/or (b) phenotypically well-established and 'pre-organized' stereotyped movement sequences will occur (see Table 1).

Whilst the actual mechanisms employed in the maintenance of typical intensity are still very little understood, the literally enormous development in the understanding of the effect of androgens on behaviour—particularly, for instance, the extraordinary localization of steroid effects in the bird's brain and the variable hypersensitivity to androgen[3]—have shown the kind of mechanisms which may well be found to be crucial in this key aspect of the functioning of fixed action patterns.

A particularly striking example of a modern study of fixed action pattern is provided by the work of Baerends and Drent[4] on the incubation of the herring gull (*Larus argentatus*) and the mechanisms of its release, orientation, and maintenance. This incubation has a stereotyped form specific to the taxonomic group in which it occurs. It is released and directed by definite external stimuli, and is influenced by internal factors fluctuating in strength. Most of the known examples of very firmly stereotyped fixed action patterns concern short-lasting activities—action patterns that, after having been released, pass off irrespective of the effect they have. Under natural conditions there is hardly any chance for the external situation to change in the period between the release and the end of the activity. But in incubation, which is a long-lasting activity, it has been shown that we have a pattern that needs not only releasing and directing stimuli for its continuation but also a regular flow of feedback stimuli 'reporting' its effect to the bird. This implies that besides fixed action patterns that run off without the apparent influence of feedback (e.g., egg retrieving) there also exist fixed motor patterns for the continuation or maintenance of which such stimuli are essential—such as incubation or the suckling act in baby mammals.

Behaviour patterns as consummatory acts

A particularly interesting aspect of the nature and function of specific action patterns is their ritualization, both in animals and man. There is abundant evidence that in the course of evolution, intention movements, displacement activity, and such like have been developed, modified, or schematized to serve as social signals or releasers for appropriate behaviour in fellow members of the species. In this way innumerable actions which were originally performed as intention movements or displacement activities have become, so to speak, translated into symbols or signal movements and thus have come to be qualified as fixed action patterns. For once an action has come to have a signal meaning it is often necessary for it to become rigid so that it may be always recognised by individuals of the same or other species as having a particular connotation. This process is what is usually meant by ritualization.[5]

As has been emphasized earlier in this book, ethologists originally paid particular attention to those fixed action patterns which often constitute an end point or climax of either major or minor chains of instinctive behaviour. The term 'consummatory act' has its counterpart, if not its origin, in much earlier writings of physiologists and psychologists. The most obvious cases of consummatory acts in the original sense are to be found in those behavioural contexts which are most intimately and directly concerned with survival and reproduction. The acts of copulation and of the ingestion of food, for instance, are acts which most obviously bring to a conclusion, at least for a while, the elaborate chains of instinctive behaviour that preceded them. Now while in both these instances the immediate physiological effects, such as the discharge of semen or the replenishment of the food reserves of the body, are obviously partly responsible for the state of satiety which follows, this is by no means always or completely the case. The very acts of picking up food, chewing, and swallowing all contribute to the assuagement of appetite and if the stomach or crop be artificially distended at the same time or if, by some other means, it is ensured that the animal receives no nutriment whatever, nevertheless the consummatory result is still maintained. That is to say that the animal appears to be 'satisfied' in much the same way and often to the same degree as it would have been had the food been consumed or normal copulation effected. Thus in experiments in which puppies are deprived of sucking experience (though adequately fed) during the first ten days of life it has been shown that the sucking reflexes are independent of hunger and food intake. The puppy still sucks even though its stomach is full of milk, and there is similar evidence suggesting that the act of sucking and the stimulus situation associated with it are consummatory in young animals as distantly related as the bottle-nosed dolphin (*Tursiops truncatus*) and the dormouse (*Muscardinus avellanarius*), the domestic cat and man himself.

Another very fertile area for the investigation of the consummatory nature of certain fixed action patterns is supplied by the study of the nesting behaviour both of birds and some mammals. Many small song birds apparently have an inborn recognition of the kind of material that should be sought for in the different periods of nest construction. Such a bird has first to gather nest material, then it must carry the material to the nest site, and then, sitting in the partly formed nest cup, build it into the structure. The fact that this innate recognition of suitable bents and grass stems as appropriate for building occurs can be shown dramatically if one rears canaries in artificial nests made of felt, so that the young birds have never encountered anything long and flexible. When these female birds themselves come to the stage of nest building, they can of course do nothing unless some material is provided. But the instant a blade of grass, a bit of string, or any long and flexible object is placed in the cage they display interest; and within seconds are carrying it to the nest place and commencing the weaving movements. When the developing nest has reached a certain point, feathers are required for lining. Again if no feathers or similar soft materials are provided the activity will cease; but the 'innate' capacity to recognise feathers as the kind of stuff with which nests 'should be lined' is dramatically illustrated by the way birds may pluck their own feathers in order to line the nest. Still more remarkable was the case, described by Hinde, of a deprived female canary which took hold of one of its own feathers in its beak, flew to the nest site in the cage without pulling out the feather, went through the motions of lining the nest with it, and then flew back to the original point in the cage from which she started—only to repeat the same performance again and again as if building an effective nest.

Similarly the brown rat possesses three motor patterns which achieve the collection and general arrangement of nesting material. Having decided upon a potential nest site, the first item of behaviour to take place is running out, grabbing nest material, carrying it back, and dropping it at the point of departure. (It is interesting to note that inexperienced rats, if deprived of all material, do exactly the same with their own tails, behaving *pari passu* as did the feather-deprived canary.) The rat's second nesting pattern consists of sitting in the nest, turning from side to side and heaping up with its forepaws a more or less circular wall of nesting material. Pattern number three involves patting the inside of the wall with the forepaws so as to tamp down and smooth the inner surface of the nest cavity. It is very interesting to note that an inexperienced rat, offered paper strips or other soft material for the first time, will go into a frenzy of all three of these activities, each of which is performed with complete perfection, not differing, even when analysed by slow-motion cinematography, from those of an experienced rat. However, the naïve rat does something the experienced rat never does: after carrying two or three paper strips which are lying flat on the ground it will perform heaping up movements in the empty air above them, even to the patting movements; tamping down the nest wall which is not yet in existence! Konrad Lorenz (1969) argues that it is the failure to get the 'rewarding reaffirmation that teaches the rat not to do the heaping movements before enough material has been carried in, and similarly not to perform the patting movements before a sufficiently high nest wall has been heaped up.'

Although we have selected fixed action patterns which come at or near the end of a chain of behavioural acts as of particular interest in that they show more clearly than most the 'drive' or 'internal pressure' behind such actions, there are nevertheless many examples of acts preliminary to the performance of the consummatory ones which are also, if only to a lesser degree, specifically driven in much the same sort of way. Yet the consummatory acts seem to be dominant in that they are capable of acting as a reinforcer for a preceding weaker response. This idea has been put forward by D. Premack[6] in his 'preponent response' theory. As a good example he mentions that the deermouse (*Peromyscus*), when studied in an apparatus so arranged that by pressing a bar it can secure the delivery of sand in the cage, will do so quite enthusiastically because the mouse 'wants' the sand, but it wants it because it provides an opportunity to dig and the digging response is an essential part of the nest-making and retreat behaviour. When we come to the higher mammals and particularly to the primates (W. A. Mason, 1965) even actions the sole function of which is to provide opportunity to play are reinforcing.

One could continue at length discussing the precise nature of the consummatory act, but I think enough has been said to show that while the concept has not the importance it had in the original corpus of ethological theorizing, it still maintains a useful function in organising these concepts and observations upon animal behaviour.

Evidences for drive

We have shown above that a very real problem is raised by the question of the motivation of particular stereotyped actions. The name used by the pioneer ethologists, following Lorenz, was 'action specific energy'. This was a thoroughly bad term and was later softened to 'specific action potential'. But the original term did, and does, refer to a real phenomenon which does not disappear by calling it 'incremental effect', 'increase in responsiveness to stimulation', etc. The increase in responsiveness is an outward sign of an internal change, and what most, if not all, ethologists want to discover is the physiological basis for such change. So the question of the internal motivation of specific acts leads us straight into the general problem of 'drives'. As was explained in an earlier part of this book the examples which bring out this problem are those which most dramatically provide evidence for the intense concentration and urgency behind behaviour patterns —urgency so strong that it can lead both the rat and the canary, and innumerable other animals, to a break out of the actual behaviour pattern, so to speak *in vacuo*. When this happens there is an overwhelming impression (with which we are often familiar from our own behaviour) of an emotional tension behind the exercise of the instinctive act. Not only does this occur in higher animals with which we may feel some personal sympathy and understanding; we see it also in invertebrates. Thus it is noteworthy in the hermit crab's behaviour as it selects the best available shell for its future habitation.[7]

The hermit crab is not (like most crabs) fully protected by a hard cuticle but has soft and vulnerable hinder segments. So it seeks out empty seashells such as those of a whelk, inserts its tail therein and lives safely protected. As it grows it becomes too large for its 'house' and so has to seek another.

When the ethologists first enunciated their 'system of instincts' there was great reluctance among the neurophysiologists to admit that the nervous system could be effecting anything like the very precise determination and direction of movements which the theory required. Now, however, all is changed, and the views of modern neurophysiologists stress rather the ubiquitous nature of central patterning. Indeed Bullock[8] stresses that 'the output of single neurons and groups of neurons is probably always patterned', and again he says, 'a whole world lies before us of integrating units that receive converging inputs, process information according to weighting factors, transfer functions, and network connections, to achieve an abstraction of certain qualities from the arriving messages'; in other words, 'recognition on predetermined criteria'.

A modern physiologist will be led to suggest that the ascending reticular system is the neural substrate associated with the 'general' aspect of drives. But as Hinde (1970) has pointed out, 'reticular activity must be between certain limits, if functionally integrated behaviour is to occur. But there is yet no satisfactory evidence that increase in recticular activity within those limits results in an increase in frequency or intensity with which a 'reticular pattern' of behaviour is shown. But it is not only the nervous system which is now seen as a much more effective instrument for controlling these fine details of instinctive behaviour; similar advances in the study of the effect of hormones show how precise and finely adjusted the hormone changes are and how quickly and delicately they control behaviour. An outstandingly good example of this is shown by the work of Hinde on the breeding behaviour of canaries (see Figure 17).

There has been much argument in the past as to whether and to what extent drives can be usefully classified as either special or general. It is quite obvious, from what has already been said, that much motivation expresses itself in the activation of particular patterns of behaviour (or at least in the activation in groups of behaviour patterns) which are functionally related in one way or another. If this is conceded, as it must be, the question can then be asked whether we should classify drives by their apparent objects and results, and if so, to what extent. Obviously there seem to be what may be called sex drives and hunger drives. Used incautiously, such assumptions, particularly expressed as they at one time were under the title of 'determining tendencies', can lead us to the supposition that almost every activity which an animal is capable of has a special drive behind it. This has led in the past to fantastic multiplication of drive states—including such absurdities as social drives, pain-avoiding drives, respiratory drives, comfort drives, self-preservatory drives, excretory drives, and so on *ad infinitum*, in absurd confusion. So we have to look not merely at the kind of action which a drive produces but also at its mechanism. If we do this, we find that while some drives are obviously specialized in their effects, it is nevertheless quite hard to find a drive, particularly if hormone secretion plays a substantial part in its make-up, which is confined in its effects to a single type of activity.

It has proved extraordinarily difficult to devise experimental

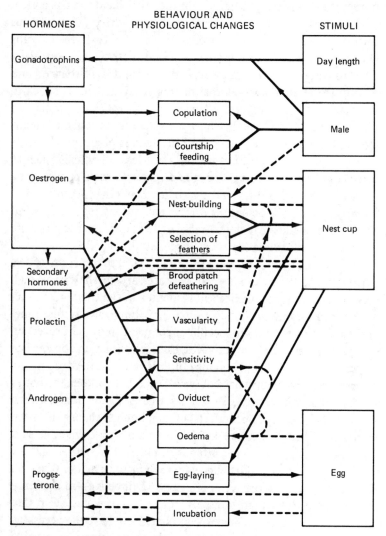

Figure 17 Breeding behaviour of canaries.

situations which show exactly how specific a drive is. But as Hinde says, 'on present evidence, the reasonable view is that, within limits, the *intensity* of any one type of behaviour *depends only on motivational factors more or less specific to it*, and others are of relatively minor importance.' On the other hand there is a great deal of evidence for a more general effect of drive. Thus various carnivores (Beach, 1947), many birds, amongst them gulls (Armstrong, 1950), and monkeys (Hinde, 1970), are especially likely to show sexual behaviour after a mild disturbance; and painful stimulation such as that arising from an electric shock to the foot can elicit fighting (Ulrich et al., 1964) or copulation (Barfield and Sachs, 1968)[9] in a considerable number of mammalian species; and of course there are factors of a general nature such as changes in temperature, which at least in animals such as insects, govern the general range and intensity of response. Ants, for instance, walk slowly and go about their other activities in a lethargic manner if the temperature is too low and may be speeded up if the temperature is slightly above the normal; so the postulate of some sort of general drive is a necessity.

As Fentress (1968) argues, to prove the extreme form of the general drive hypothesis it will be necessary to show that each motivational factor influences all responses to some extent. But an animal can do only a limited number of things at any one time, and so a supposedly non-specific effect could only be proved by observation of all specific activities, each in a situation appropriate to it, and, as Hinde (1970) points out, it is rare that the proponents of a general drive theory have observed even two different activities in the same experiment. It follows that a distinction between specific and non-specific effects of a stimulus change is often extremely difficult to draw, and I agree with Hinde when he says that the question is more profitably phrased in terms of how specific or how general the effects on each factor may be. While all the components of a drive can of course be directive—in the sense of a mechanism adapted to a particular goal—it would seem that only the central nervous system component can have the necessary complexities of structure to enable it to originate or provide anything that appears to go beyond the limits of mere directiveness and to approach the appearance of intelligent purposiveness. When we see how intimately interlocked are visceral, hormonal, and central nervous system factors in internal drive we realise that such internal drives are something much more complicated, at least in most cases, than mere visceral stimulation. So the present picture is one of an internal drive in the form of patterns of activity in the central nervous system which can be the result either of visceral stimulation or of hormonal stimulation, or can be truly endogenous in the sense of originating within the nervous system itself (see Adrian, 1950, for the pioneer observations).

Bullock (1961, 1966) shows how such a variety of examples of nervous organization for controlling behaviour are now neurophysiologically established, mainly in the invertebrates; and that we have ample factual evidence for the existence of neuronal devices which, singly and in co-operation, can account for all postulated types of organized behaviour: from behaviour of the highest degree of fixity on the one hand to extreme flexibility on the other, and from systems exhibiting complete peripheral initiation and control to those where this control is exclusively central.

Displacement activity: drive gone astray?

A classic view of displacement activities, in Chapter 1, was linked with hierarchical concepts of drive as put forward by Tinbergen and Kortlandt. This, while not essentially incorrect, has been developed and modified a great deal by recent research. It is now realised that some cases of displacement activity can be accounted for as a result of autonomic activity aroused by frightening stimuli or other aspects of the environmental situation. An example of this is the cooling responses shown by buntings (*Emberizidae*) in sexual chases, when the autonomic activity engendered by the conflict situation also provides stimuli for somatic activities which appear at first sight to be irrelevant. For example, vasomotor or pilomotor activity may provide skin stimuli which, in their turn, elicit scratching or preening. Similarly dryness of the throat may elicit drinking. Then there is the disinhibition hypothesis. In some examples of conflict mutual incompatibility may prevent the appearance of those types of behaviour which would otherwise have the highest priority; and so patterns which would otherwise have been suppressed are able to appear. Thus Andrew (1956) pointed out that the displacement preening which buntings show in conflict situations can be regarded as a consequence of peripheral stimuli which normally induce preening but whose effect is easily inhibited by the factors for other activities. In a conflict situation these other activities cannot occur and preening is possible.

A great deal of evidence about preening activities of birds fits into this general view. The theory has, for instance, been applied to terns (*Chlidonias*) and to the chaffinch (*Fringilla coelebs*) (van Iersel and Bol, 1958; Rowell, 1961). These authors again lay emphasis on external stimulation, assuming that some degree of stimulation for preening is always present. A word of caution is necessary here; Hinde (1970, p. 409) points out that the presence of external stimulation for preening is normally revealed only by the occurrence of preening—preening is, however, augmented by increasing the external stimuli.

Equally good if not better evidence in support of inhibition has been provided by the three-spined stickleback (*Gasterosteus aculeatus*) by Sevenster (1961).[10] For mammals another important study is that of Fentress (1968) on the grooming of voles. He produces partial support for the disinhibition hypothesis in that after a frightening stimulus these animals flee and/or freeze, groom their fur, then walk around or continue with other maintenance activities. Apparently irrelevant grooming therefore occurs in the transitional state between freezing and/or fleeing and the other types of behaviour. As a result of a comprehensive study Fentress suggests that this disinhibition hypothesis accounts for the overall occurrence of grooming but may need to be supplemented by further considerations. Thus some of the earlier results of brain stimulation in the cockerel with implanted electrodes (von Holst and von St Paul, 1963) showed, in one series of experiments, that stimulation by one electrode caused fleeing, and that by the other, sleep. When hungry, the elicitation of a slight fleeing tendency causes a bird to stop eating. If, however, the 'sleeping stimulus' is given, the animal may feed briefly before sleeping. So the authors ascribe this to the liberation of feeding when sleeping inhibits fleeing.

The general conclusion arising from this work is that displacement activities cannot always be sharply distinguished from the same activities appearing in their normal functional context. There seems a good deal of evidence that displacement activities tend to occur not only at the point of balance in an approach-avoidance conflict, but also at other change-over points. Besides the examples mentioned above, useful evidence is supplied by grooming in the rat, comfort movements in sticklebacks, etc.

As an interim summary of the situation, we can say that, in spite of objections to the original formulation of the displacement theory, it is quite obvious that many display movements have been derived, not from patterns associated with the major conflicting tendencies but from *apparently* irrelevant activities such as preening, incubating, and so on. If the movements are incomplete we find some overlap between the categories. In birds the commonest examples are bill-wiping and preening movements, which have been elaborated into complex displays in some species. Similarly in some fishes the movements used in shaking off ectoparasites have curiously become part of the male courting ritual.[11] So we see that displacement activities take their place, and an important one, in the study of what might be called the micro-evolution of behaviour as illustrated by the evolutionary development of avian display. Here the classic paper of Konrad Lorenz on the *Anatinae* (1941), referred to earlier in this book, provides a marvellously coherent argument which shows how comparison of behavioural characters can provide evidence about the course of their evolution. So displacement activities, fixed action patterns, intention movements, and autonomic responses all have their place in modern views as to the mechanism of evolution of displays characteristic of different but related species (see Chapter 2).

Releasers: keys for opening sluices

Any consideration of the nature of drive, particularly, of course, of internal drive, brings us straight up against the problem of releasers. In what sense does a drive need releasing, and how is this release accomplished? Obviously it is accomplished by external stimulation; but why are the effects of stimuli so specialized, so strange, and how has selective responsiveness to them

Table 2. Some studies indicating differential responsiveness to aspects of the natural stimulus object for species-characteristic responses.[12]

Species	Response	Characters of major importance	Characters of minor importance	Reference
Silkworm	Male's approach to female	Specific smell of female	Other smells	Butenandt, 1955
Water-beetle (Dytiscus)	Prey-catching	Chemical and tactile stimuli	Visual characters Visual stimuli	Tinbergen, 1951
Grayling butterfly (Eumenis semele)	Male sexual pursuit	Dark shade Type of movement Distance	Shape	Tinbergen et al., 1943
Fritillary butterfly (Argynnis paphia)	Male sexual pursuit	Colour Speed of flicker Size	Black patterning Shape	Magnus, 1958
Mantis	Prey-catching	Distance Type of movement	Size, shape, direction, colour, smell	Rilling et al., 1959
Honey-bee worker	Food-begging	Head carrying specific scent Tactile stimuli from antennae	Body Colour and shape of head	Free, 1956
Honey-bee worker	Stinging	Dark colour Sting venom odour Human sweat odour Movement	General bee odour	Free, 1961

Species	Behaviour	Sign stimuli		References
Char (*Salmo alpinus*)	Attack; Nest-site selection	Red colour; Visual stimuli from gravel	Size, shape; Tactile stimuli from gravel	Fabricius and Gustafson, 1954
Darter (*Etheostoma blennioides*)	Egg-laying	Texture	Smell; Colour	Winn, 1957
Cichlid fish (*Apistogramma* sp.)	Approach to parent by young	Movement; Colour	Form; Size	Kuenzer and Kuenzer, 1962 (see also Kühme, 1962)
Turkey	Fleeing from a winged predator	Relation between speed and size	Shape	Schleidt, 1961
Domestic hen	Maternal protection of chicks	Distress call	Visual characters	Müller, 1961; Brückner, 1933
Domestic hen	Mounting	Crouching posture	Male and female characters	Fisher and Hale, 1956; 1957 (see also Carbaugh *et al.*, 1962)
Brewer blackbird (*Euphagus cyanocephalus*)	Male mating behaviour	Posture; Head and/or tail above horizontal; Colour of foreparts	Eye colour; Colour of posterior region; Wings	Howell and Bartholomew, 1952
Bullfinch (*Pyrrhula pyrrhula*)	Anxiety responses	Visual texture; Convex surface; Coloured surface	Specific outline of predator	Kramer and von St Paul, 1951
Herring gull; White mouse	Egg-rolling; Retrieving of young by inexperienced female	Speckling, size, colour; Cries of young	Shape; Visual and olfactory characteristics of drowned young	Baerends, 1957, 1959; Noirot, 1964

come about? Examples of such releasers in the early classical papers of ethology are so widely known as to require no detailed description. Such instances are the red belly of the male stickle-back, the red breast of the robin, the spot on the tip of a gull's bill, etc. Table 2 is useful in indicating the variety of differential responsiveness to different aspects of the natural world which the animal encounters.

To account for this selectiveness classical ethology invoked the concept of an innate releasing mechanism (I.R.M.) largely, if not entirely, inborn. This included a receptory correlate ensuring that the young animal at least pays attention to the particular stimuli in its environment which are likely to be of significance—assuming that both mechanisms are, in varying degrees, adjustable by experience. One particular feature of the animal's response to a releaser was its ability to perform what was called *heterogenous summation*. Thus, where a response is influenced by several charac-ters of the stimulus, either through different sensory modalities or by the same one, the effects may supplement each other. In the case of experiments on the Grayling butterfly (*Eumenis semele*), the sexual pursuit by the male is influenced by the type of movement shown by the model, by the darkness of its colour, and by its distance. Deficiencies in any one of the stimulus characters can be compensated for by increasing one of the others; a pale model close by is as effective as a dark model at a distance. This 'law' sometimes applies qualitatively to individually conditioned or learned responses as well as to species characteristic ones. But Hinde (1970) points out that in its strongest form it would imply that the total number of responses released by the parts of the stimulus presented successively is the same as the number released by the whole. This is clearly contrary to the view, basic to *gestalt* psychology, which is so often baldly stated as 'the whole is more than the sum of its parts'. It has accordingly been sug-gested that the differences may be one of phyletic level, hetero-genous summation applying at lower levels of organization and the *gestalt* principle in more highly evolved organisms—and there is indeed a lot to be said in favour of this solution of the apparent conflict.[13]

There may also be a change with age—the law of heterogenous summation being important in the first period of life but its role decreasing with age and sensory experience. A striking example of this (which needs further study) is given by Bower.[14] In this experiment human infants were trained to turn their heads when the stimulus was presented—the reinforcement being a fifteen-second 'peek-a-boo' from an experimenter. When the response rate had reached criterion, generalization was assessed by presenting the condition stimulus with its parts for fifteen-second periods in counterbalanced order until extinction was complete. The results gave surprisingly exact confirmation of the theory. With eight- to twelve-week-old infants, the law was obviously holding precisely but at sixteen and twenty weeks the whole was found to produce more responses than the sum of those produced by its parts. So we see that the law of heterogenous summation is still of great value; but very little can usefully be said about the internal mechanisms which mediate its action. When we come to discuss perception we shall see that the fast accumulating body of neurological evidence produced by great technical expertise in single-unit recording, though resulting in many significant advances in knowledge, has not yet reached the stage at which it impinges significantly on the kinds of experiment which ethologists carry out.

Stimulus selection

A particularly valuable ethological study of stimulus selection has been provided by G. P. Baerends and J. P. Kruijt entitled 'Stimulus Selection'.[15] The paper is the result of comparison in gulls of the relative value of various components of the stimulus situations releasing and directing a number of different responses, and confirms the original idea, implied in the I.R.M. concept, that physically identical stimuli may be evaluated differently by an animal according to the activity they are controlling. Their evidence suggests that this evaluation takes place in a series of steps.

The first step concerns the release of activity among the sensory cells; in further steps, located more centrally in the sensory pathways but not necessarily all outside the receptor organ, the output of the receptors is processed in analysers or evaluating units. Finally heterogenous summation of the output of these units takes place before the motor mechanisms are triggered. As a result of the data on colour it seems the analyser (i.e., the yellow-green code, or its mirror image the red–blue code) can be used by different responses. This suggests that it is not the information processors themselves but the pathway through which the relevant information flows, that is specific for the response. The common use of analysers for incompatible responses implies that conflicts are possible when the internal factors facilitating these responses are simultaneously activated. Simultaneous activation of the tendencies to incubate and to flee led to a compromise in which incubation responses were directed towards objects sub-optimal to both responses. In the cases studied the rule of heterogenous summation has been found to apply independently of whether the stimulus response attachment perceived was learnt or not.

The phenomenon of supernormal stimuli may occur even in cases where no influence of learning on the stimulus-response attachments can be found; and so there is little doubt that, at least in some cases, the experiments on the supernormal stimulus (e.g., the attractiveness of eggs larger than normal, of eggs more strikingly marked than normal; or, in the Grayling butterfly, the greater effectiveness of ultra-large or ultra-dark models for the male insects' sexual pursuit flight) show summation amongst the 'innate' elements which make up the I.R.M.

This would seem an appropriate place to refer to the long-standing controversy concerning the use of the term 'innate' and to refer to behaviour as *either* innate *or* learned. The way in which any reference to what may be called the nature-nurture controversy has aroused, and continues to arouse, passionate conflict, particularly in relation to human life, is curious. There are, no doubt, deep psychological and sociological reasons for this which need not concern us here, but it is indeed strange that much controversy of this type bedevilled the early stages of ethology long before it began to approach the active consideration of human behaviour.

The four traditionally assumed characteristics of instincts are that instinct is primarily (a) inherited, (b) patterned in form,

(c) adaptive, and (d) endogenous in the sense of being of internal origin. Enough has already been said in this book to provide examples of all these characteristics. It seems however that the controversy is very largely centred round the tendency to make a rigid distinction between behaviour which is instinctive on the one hand and behaviour which is learned on the other. Now this sharp distinction *can* lead to erroneous conclusions and fruitless argument since it is obvious that a great deal of behaviour that is governed to a large extent by the genetic make-up of the animal may also be greatly affected by experience. So it is far more useful to consider whether a given item of behaviour is 'environmentally stable' on the one hand or 'environmentally labile' on the other. Indeed items of behaviour may vary greatly in this respect within a single species—some of them clearly falling into one category, others into another.

But while it is true enough that the animal, even in the egg or womb, is exposed to variations in environmental conditions just as it is after it is hatched or born, biologically speaking there is no sharper distinction amongst the phases of a life history than that between the first phase in the egg or the uterus and the free-living second phase—when the creature's senses are all becoming active and are being exposed to environmental stimuli of every conceivable kind.

To assume that there is no interaction between external factors and internal ones is ridiculous; it implies no interaction between hereditary information and acquired information. No one, not even the most rabid exponents of the instinct *versus* learning argument, ever supposed any such thing. It follows that the argument of Hebb, that to ask how much a given piece of behaviour depends on genetic factors and how much on environmental, is as meaningless as to ask how much the area of a field depends on its length and how much on its width—because if the field had no length or no width it would have no area. And an organism can neither be without a genome nor without an environment. But the field would have an area (although we should not call it a field) if it were 1 mm wide and twenty kilometres long, and it might well be that in an organism an overwhelming proportion of the instructions which determine its make-up and activity come from one source and a miniscule amount from another. A highly impervious cyst or the chorion of an insect egg effectively protects the organism from the major environmental influences (exceptions include those of temperature and oxygen supply). Indeed the structure of the cyst wall or egg-shell seems specifically designed to eliminate external influences to the utmost possible degree. Let us suppose for the sake of argument that, as in the development of a nematode worm, or a springtail (Collembolan), the form and capacity of the hatching organism is little different from that of the same organism when it is ready to reproduce. In this case it seems entirely reasonable to assume that the features of the organism are mainly determined by its hereditary constitution and extremely slightly, and only in a very general way, influenced by abnormalities or changes in the environment.

Another curious confusion which has given rise to much unnecessary argument is the assertion that the word innate can only be defined in negative terms! And this has often been bolstered by the assumption that it is impossible to say anything positive about the genetics of inheritance because, 'what is genetically determined is the difference between one organism and another'. To restrict the role and scope of genetics in this way is quite inadmissible—for the simple reason that in one sense all science, and indeed all perception, is based on the study of differences. If you cannot detect the difference between them, you cannot say anything about the relationship of two cells, two organs, or two pieces of behaviour. What in fact genetics is, and always has been, doing is to study and interpret the factors which govern the development of complexity in the early stages of the development of an organism, and to attempt to understand the manner in which these qualities and abilities are passed on to the next generation. As I have suggested above, we often detect the 'innateness' of behaviour patterns by seeing how far their forms of complexity and adaptiveness can be determined by practice or example. But this does not mean that the definition of innateness is negative, because we also have to determine how highly organized, highly elaborate, how adaptive is the rest of the behaviour—

and this determination is as positive as anything else to be learned about the complexities of organizations.

It must also be remembered that since the 'classical' period there has been an immense development in knowledge of the processes of growth and maturation in the mammalian nervous system during the pre-adult life. This is far too technical and complicated to be reviewed in a book such as this; suffice it to say that cell division and migration and neuro-differentiation in the central nervous system are of the first importance. In the cerebellum there are inherent growth mechanisms which underlie locomotive behaviour and similarly in the cerebral cortex—both motor, prefrontal, and visual—important developmental changes in extrinsic connexions and organization of the central nervous systems occur. Finally, in the limbic system there are also many examples of plasticity in development. All these and similar advances will ultimately have to be taken into account in any full assessment of the basis and course of innate behaviour.[16]

Imprinting

Let us now consider imprinting, a subject which has such broad implications for the study of behaviour, particularly for the relationship between intrinsic and extrinsic factors, that it could have been introduced at almost any point in the present account. However, it provides a convenient bridge between the releasers which we have just been discussing and the major problem still to be dealt with: the nature of perception and its characteristics in relation to the animal's adjustment to its environments.

As we have seen, the classic examples of imprinting, i.e., learning which results from the young animal following a parent, go back at least to the late nineteenth century. At first it was thought (see, for example, Heinroth, 1910) that the learning in this situation was fundamentally different from other forms of learning —as the nature of learning was then understood. It is now realised that some of the properties of imprinting arise from the particular conditions of the following situation, and there is perhaps no reason to consider imprinting as being fundamentally different from other forms of learning. Imprinting was originally defined by four characteristics: (a) learning confined to a very definite and brief section of the individual's early life; (b) learning which once established is often very stable and in some cases perhaps irreversible; (c) as a process which, though completed early, later in the life cycle affects various specific reactions as yet undeveloped—such as those concerned with sexual and adult social behaviour; and (d) learning which is generalized in the sense that it leads first to an ability to respond to the broad characteristics of the situation, yet later may enable finer discriminations to be achieved. All these four characteristics are important and each applies in at least some cases, but from the present-day point of view the sensitive period and progression from general to special perception are perhaps the most important. The former involves the educational question of sensitive periods in learning, and the latter ties up with an equally basic topic, namely observational and exploratory learning.

The learning which takes place in the classical imprinting situation, where young birds learn to follow the first large moving object they see, enables the young first to recognise the overall appearances of the parent species as the 'right' object to follow, and later to recognise the parent as distinct from all other individuals. Following behaviour, similar to that characteristic of imprinting in birds, can be observed in young mammals that risk being separated early from their parents. But it is much less common in mammals whose young spend longer in the nest, probably because they are primarily creatures whose sense of smell is highly developed, and it is this sense which is most likely to be dominant in establishing mother–offspring and sibling relations.

In some examples the limitations of the sensitive period is remarkable. Amongst chicks and mallard ducklings imprinting is most effective between thirteen and sixteen hours after hatching. Thus chicks will not follow a novel moving object, for instance a man, when they are only a few hours old; nor when they are several days old, but only during the crucial intervening period. Moreover, the intensity of the sensitive period may be different for related species. Even in a single species, the sensitive periods for auditory and visual stimuli may differ.

It appears today that imprinting consists largely of the development of familiarity with moving objects. Specific rewards, such as food or contact with a moving object or model, are not necessary. Under ordinary barnyard conditions chicks become familiar with at least two types of moving object: the mother and the siblings. Under experimental conditions, coots (*Fulica atra*), for instance, can learn to follow several different objects. If familiarity is the main issue then imprinting would seem to be closely related to perceptual learning, for in both cases responsiveness to a stimulus is influenced by a previous experience with a stimulus independent of its association with any reward. Bateson has shown that imprinting can be a valuable tool for investigating the genesis of perceptual aspects of behaviour—for any learning during the sensitive period may be revealed in contexts other than in the following response. Thus he found that the performance of chicks in a discrimination problem is improved when one of the patterns to be discriminated is the same as that on the walls of the home pen. He also observed that early imprinting to a flickering light (visual flicker) facilitates teaching the animal to avoid the same stimulus a month later. This effect was apparent, however, only in those individuals that exhibited the following response with a stimulus during the imprinting period, which suggests that mere exposure to the stimulus is not sufficient for the early perceptual learning to occur. Thus it may be necessary for the stimulus to become associated with a response of some kind although it does not have to be the same response used in subsequent testing to reveal perceptual learning.

The conclusion that, during the sensitive period, conspicuous objects have a reinforcing effectiveness upon naïve birds which seems to increase with familiarity, is consistent with many of the findings of imprinting experiments. For instance, an imprinted bird shows searching behaviour when the object is absent; in addition the willingness to follow an object and respond to it selectively tends to increase with experience. The evidence also indicates that reward is unnecessary for imprinting, and that objects which at first invoke fear may later, after habituation and familiarity, elicit following responses. Moreover, unfamiliar objects are more likely to elicit following when presented in the same situation in which the bird has previously been imprinted to other objects.

The literature on imprinting is now very large, and is still growing. Perhaps the best recent summary of the topic is that provided by P. P. G. Bateson on 'Internal influences in early learning in birds'.[17] Bateson's review covers selective responsiveness, the sensitive period, behavioural influences on acquisition of the imprinting response, and the consequences of the attachment process. His review highlights two general points with regard to the early perceptual development in birds. Firstly, it is clear that the internal influences on what can be learned are diverse. Some of these, such as selective responses to particular stimuli, set limits on what can be learnt and can be described unambiguously as constraints. Others, such as the bird's active seeking for stimuli of a certain type before and during the attachment process, suggest that the course of perceptual learning is in part *controlled* by events occurring inside the animal. The second general issue brought out by this work is that an internal influence is not necessarily and exclusively genetically determined. Bateson considers it probable, though not yet established, that the initial preferences and the specific form of the initial behaviour shown by the young birds are determined only by genetic factors, even though non-specific environmental influences play a part in the development of the preference and the patterning of social and repetitive behaviour. However, the consequences of experience in the imprinting situation undoubtedly have a major effect on subsequent learning processes. What is more, the specific experience interacts with the pre-existing organization of the animal's behaviour and can thus produce unexpected results. He stresses that the relationship between the internal influences on learning and the processes involved in their development are far from straightforward, but he concludes, 'the lesson is, then, that the issue of what constrains and controls learning should not be confused with the question of how these constraints and controls were specified earlier in the development.'

A type of learning in birds which in many respects is similar to that of the learning that occurs in the following situation, is perceptual learning shown by birds, especially song-birds, in the early acquisition of the characteristic vocalizations of the species and their use for individual recognition. A general summary of this, by Thorpe, will be found in *Non-Verbal Communication*.[18] In this matter of imitative learning of songs, the order in which the behaviour pattern is developed may be important; for example, exploration of the environment may be disastrous if it occurs before the young animal has established some standards of what is familiar. In such cases acquisition of information must precede performance. This is particularly obvious in the development of complex motor patterns which are at the basis of the ability of a bird to sing its song correctly.[19] If the song is to be finely tuned to match some predetermined pattern (which may or may not be learned), feedback from the performance must be compared with the preferred value. Once a motor pattern producing the appropriate feedback has been established, dependence on feedback can be reduced or even eliminated and the animal can accelerate the output rate. As Bateson points out, this is rather like a musician learning a new part. While he has to monitor the individual sounds he is making to ensure their accuracy, he must allow at least 100 ms between each note. However, in the final performance when such control is no longer needed, the gaps between notes can be greatly reduced to 50 ms or even less.[20]

Perception

It is clear that several of the subjects dealt with in the preceding paragraphs involve, in an acute and critical way, the general topic of perceptual abilities. One can say at once that ethological work over the last twenty years or more has contributed an immense amount to our knowledge and understanding of vision, hearing, proprioception (including spatial perception and orientation), chemoperception (taste and smell), temperature perception, time perception, perception of gravity, and the perception of electric currents and of magnetism. To discuss adequately even a tithe of these topics in this book is manifestly impossible. As an example, perception and kindred topics occupy approximately a hundred pages in Hinde's book (1970) in which the whole field is far from covered, and an enormous amount of new knowledge has resulted from the research of the last seven years. Accordingly I wish merely to point out some of the areas of research which have produced modern results, and to see if they give any helpful suggestions as to the future development of ethological studies.

Most of the outstandingly new conclusions arise naturally from the study of animal communication and long-distance orientation. Amongst these I would specify the migratory and homing orientation of birds, the auditory orientation of bats, fish, whales, and some birds, by echo-location. Perhaps above all, the discovery of the complexities of pattern recognition and preference shown by those animals and groups which have highly developed visual and auditory organs, particularly the birds, the bats, and in some respects the insects (as exemplified by the honey bee), and the development of perceptual analysis among the primates, has arisen from the study of communication.

All these topics are essentially linked by their importance in relation to pattern perception, both visual and auditory, and by the fact that they have extended very greatly our knowledge of the range and precision of the sense organs, such as the auditory system of birds and bats, the precision of time sense in both these groups and the rapidly mounting evidence for something akin to language in the human sense—in these and indeed in the honey bee.

One such example is the auditory system in bats. Recent work in this group has established the existence of a synthesis of auditory perception of a degree and quality hitherto unimagined. The classic work on the bat echo-location system whereby the bat not merely orients itself but even perceives, identifies, and catches flying insect prey in the dark by means of the echoes from its own supersonic cries being reflected into its ears, was performed by D. R. Griffin in the late 1950s and well into the 1960s; some of his most remarkable work in this field was published in 1967. This has since been followed up by many other able workers.[21]

The discovery that many bats use a type of biological sonar system naturally gave rise to much speculation about the mechanisms underlying this remarkable mode of orientation. The general consensus of opinion, based upon both field and laboratory evidence, is that the bat somehow retains information from the outgoing sonar cry and compares it with information from returning echoes. It was suggested that there may be a neural 'template' for storing the original transmission. Moreover, in determining the distance to the targets, echo-locating bats may perform an operation equivalent to remembering virtually all of the waveform of the outgoing cry; or the bats may use a more limited amount of potential information available from the outgoing and returning signals. This is a highly technical and rapidly developing field of research. However, there is already evidence that one group of bats using purely frequency-modulated signals has overcome the Doppler-ranging error inherent in such signals by shaping the transmitted signal so as to minimize these errors. Another group of bats using constant frequency combined with frequency modulation appears to overcome the error due to the Doppler effect by separately measuring target velocity in another functionally distinct sonar system. One species of *Rhinolophus* uses sonar cries of a duration of about 35 ms at a constant frequency of approximately 83 kHz followed by a descending sweep from this constant frequency to a frequency of 65 to 70 kHz. These cries are relatively narrow in bandwidth and the sweep covers about 15kHz around a central figure of roughly 75 kHz. In other cases, if a target is moving relatively towards the bat, the echo frequency is raised and the bat decreases the frequency of its transmission by approximately the same amount. If a target is moving away from the bat, the Doppler shift is downward, and the bat responds by raising the frequency in the constant-frequency portion of the cry. So it appears that one function of the constant frequency portion is to measure target velocity and consequent echo Doppler shift.[22] Neurophysiological research strongly indicates that the neural mechanism for cross-correlating outgoing cries and returning echoes is located in an auditory centre (inferior colliculus) which is unusually enlarged in bats.

To continue with the perception of what may be called auditory gestalten, we return to the birds. Here again the capacity of the bird auditory system is indeed impressive. Although they possess hearing organs which are in some respects inferior to ours and in others markedly superior, they may in either case show a capacity for organizing their auditory perception and their vocalizations with the precision exceeded only by man and seldom even approached by other mammals (except the bats).

The variability of vocalizations of birds is adapted, primarily by genetic programming and secondarily by imitative adjustments, to distinguish the birds' own species from every other species, and to distinguish one individual more or less certainly from all others in a population. The song of some species (for example the chaffinch (*Fringilla coelebs*)) can be so precisely controlled and adjusted by limited use of the imitative faculty, that the song can serve both functions at the same time and local dialects may arise as a by-product of the mechanism of development (see Figures 15 and 16). In species such as sea-birds which nest in dense colonies, there seems to be little group distinctiveness, but the considerable advantage which recognition based on acoustic signals offers, as against visual recognition, especially under the difficult conditions imposed by life in dense colonies on the sea shore, seems clear.[23] Neurophysiology is as yet not very far advanced in the study of bird hearing; and even in the bats the neurophysiological picture at present available by no means provides a full explanation of understanding of the powers of perceptual synthesis. In birds we find that the neurophysiology available is at present quite inadequate to this task and it is remarkable how well the principles of gestalt psychology, which were originally developed in the relation to visual-form perception, can be applied successfully to temporal forms in auditory perceptions of birds. One of the most striking examples of this is the ability of birds to display melodic transposition—the ultimate criterion for the auditory perception of 'wholes'—this is found in the songs of a number of species. Still more remarkable is the evidence for error detection and correction by the blackbird (*Turdus merula*), as further evidence for gestalt perception in birds.[24] Such results from the study of bird vocalizations have of course been dependent upon the development of high quality tape-recording and machines for analysis (such as the sound spectrograph and the melograph). The old belief in the song-bird's superior hearing was partly due to the fact that man cannot recognise rapid frequency and amplitude modulations, which are so common in bird vocalizations, but this has now been made possible by modern technical developments. But there is clear evidence that the song-bird's ear can register such sounds and that its temporal resolution is better than that of the human ear by an approximate factor of 10.[25]

The recognition of complex visual patterns both by mammals and birds has been the subject of many investigations. The neurophysiological study of this area of perception has advanced greatly in recent years, but is still a long way from rendering unnecessary the classical interpretation as expressed in the gestalt theory. This interpretation is still a useful concept and will remain so until the new physiological discoveries have reached the level at which they can be integrated more fully with a study of the perceptual abilities of the whole animal.

The central proposition of modern neurophysiological study is that our perceptions are caused by the activity of a rather small number of neurons selected from a very large population of predominantly silent cells. The activity of each single cell is thus an important perceptual event and it is supposed, as a provisional hypothesis, that the subtlety and sensitivity of perception results from the mechanisms determining when a cell becomes active, rather than from complex combinatory rules of usage of nerve cells. The original concept, according to Müller's doctrine of specific nerve energies, was of a simple mapping from sense organ to sensorium so that a copy of the physical events of the body surface was presented to the brain. The neighbouring receptive fields and modalities were also known to overlap, but when the activity of neurons at higher levels in sensory pathways was recorded, it became obvious that something was happening more complex and significant than could be fitted into the concept of simple mapping with overlap and adaptation.

From the original classic work (summarized by Hubel and Wiesel) on the eye of the frog it appeared that the properties of the retina are such that a ganglion cell can, figuratively speaking, reach out and determine that something specific is happening in front of the eye. Light is, of course, the agent by which it does this, but it is the detailed pattern of light that carries the information, and the overall level of illumination prevailing at the time is almost totally disregarded. These key patterns, or trigger features, are transmitted as a map to intermediate agents, thus allowing the higher centres to perform their tasks. This work of Hubel and Wiesel (1959) showed examples of selectivity for pattern in the responsiveness of different varieties of cells in the visual cortex of cats. They found that a light or dark line or a dark-light border was required to evoke a vigorous response in even the simplest first-order cells. Furthermore, the stimulus had to be at a rather precise orientation and position in the visual field, and often had to be moving in a specific direction. It was this scheme, in essence a hierarchical one, which gave us an indication as to how higher levels of categorization are developed from lower levels. Thus the main function of line and edge detectors discovered by Hubel and Wiesel may be to link together information about the same object in the two retinal images in order to determine the object's distance from the animal. This seems to show that at low levels the visual information is carried by the patterns of joint activity of many elements, whereas at the upper levels of the hierarchy a relatively small proportion are active and each of these says a lot *when* it is active.[26]

According to one view, only about 1000 active neurons are needed to represent the visual scene. If this is so, each neuron must convey a far greater share of the picture than, say, one point out of the quarter million points of a television picture. Barlow suggests that 'perhaps a better analogy is to recall the thousand words a picture is proverbially worth; apparently an active neuron says something of the order of complexity of a word.' He suggests that it is not unreasonable to suppose that a single visual scene can be represented quite completely by about 1000 of such entities, each equal to a word—bearing in mind that each one is selected from a vast vocabulary and will in addition carry some precisional information. But there is much physiological evidence, both old and new, which favours the rejection of the view that individual cells play an important role in perception.[27] Something like a holographic scheme is favoured.

The main argument, and an old one, levelled against the idea that individual cells play an important role in perception is that large parts of the cortex can be damaged with only minor resultant changes in behaviour or learning; and it was this that led to Lashley's doctrine of cerebral mass action. But repetition of the original experiments and refinements in methods of testing, some of it by Lashley himself, has somewhat weakened the original evidence in its favour.[28]

So we reach a curious impasse. In one aspect the organization of the visual system appears hierarchical. Yet Sherrington in his famous book *Man on his Nature* (1941) introduced the notion of 'one ultimate pontifical nerve cell . . . the climax of the whole system of integration', but immediately rejected the idea in favour of the concept of mind as a 'million-fold democracy whose each unit is a cell'. Barlow suggests that the whole of subjective experience at any one time must correspond to a specific combination of active cells, and the 'pontifical cell' should be replaced by a number of 'cardinal cells'. He suggests that 'among the many cardinals only a few speak at once; each makes a complicated statement, but not, of course, as complicated as that of the pontiff if he were to express the whole of perception in one utterance.' Here too there are difficulties. As Barlow puts it, 'if one uses the term cardinal cell, one must be sure to remember that the college of these cardinals outnumbers the church members and must include a substantial fraction of the 10^{10} cells of the human brain'. So it seems that any hierarchical organization must be duplicated to a vast degree in the nervous system—for if it were not so, Lashley's objection would certainly still apply. And as Barlow again suggests, a computer would not usually survive brain surgery or gunshot wounds. So the implications of the relative immunity of the cortex to quite extensive injury are to be taken very seriously.

It may be useful to indicate here the varieties of retinal ganglion cells which can act as detectors and have actually been found. These include sustained-contrast detectors which respond to the edge of an object lighter or darker than the background. Moving-edge detectors responding to a moving edge whether dark on light, or light on dark. Net-dimming detectors responding to a reduction in illumination. Absolute darkness detectors which discharge more rapidly the darker it is and finally (in the frog) a type of detector with a receptory field having a diameter corresponding to that of the retinal image of a fly, when the insect is at an optimum catching distance from the frog (frequently called a 'bug detector'). To return from the frog to the mammals, similar principles of organization have been found in the visual cortex, though here they seem to be far more complex. Thus mammals have units responding to shape (such as elongated images), orientation, direction of movement, and other features.

As Fabricius[29] points out, there exist neural mechanisms which could well be capable of decoding complex sets of stimuli, such as those presented by the ripe male stickleback, e.g. 'horizontally oriented oval objects with red underneath'.

But clearly, fascinating though they are, these results must yet be a very long way both in complexity and in time from guiding or even influencing the ethologist's study of visual releasers and other similar topics.

Earlier ideas as to the basically hierarchical nature of behavioural mechanisms ran into difficulties when it was found that they did not seem to fit current simplistic concepts concerning the nature of energy flow. But hierarchical concepts have proved essential in most if not all fields of biology; and R. Dawkins (*Growing Points in Ethology*, Eds. Bateson, P. P. G. and Hinde, R. A., 1976) has shown with great clarity that a hierarchical model based on the idea of 'decision making' can provide powerful explanatory concepts, akin to the rules of human syntax. Thus it is suggested that animals may initially take global decisions (as we do ourselves) and then proceed to progressively narrower sub-decisions, which eventually end up with an observed act. And such an approach certainly seems peculiarly appropriate to modern work on the behaviour of primates.

So let us return to aspects of the conceptual synthesis of which such animals are capable. Recent and continuing experiments on the language learning of apes have now produced adequate confirmation of many of the chimpanzee's most astonishing achievements. This is an important question because it relates to the arguments put forward by Chomsky and others that the possession of language is indubitable evidence of mentality and of some basic and innate mental structure without which the acquisition of true language and its purposive use, whether by animals or men, is inconceivable. These five categories of mental structure, all of which have now been fully authenticated, are as follows. In order to demonstrate the use of language the animal must be able to (a) demonstrate an extensive system of names for objects in the environment; (b) make signs about objects which are not physically present; (c) use signs for concepts, not just objects, actions, and agents; (d) invent semantically appropriate combinations; and (e) use correct order when it is semantically necessary.

The point which researchers have currently reached at the time of writing is well illustrated by recent work by D. M. Rumbaugh, entitled 'Language Learning by a Chimpanzee: the Lana Project,' as summarized by Harold T. P. Hayes.

'While the understanding of human langauge has been in the main the objective of most of these studies, the psychologists' results have yielded data so rich and unexpected that their work has come to be followed closely by biologists of several specialities, expecially neurology, and by anthropologists and philosophers of science, here and abroad. From the studies in progress, five of the chimpanzees have achieved first-name celebrity: Washoe, the best known (Oklahoma); Sarah (U.S.C.); Lana (Yerkes); Lucy (Oklahoma); and Nim (Columbia). Separately, and in some instances collectively, these animals have demonstrated the ability to converse with humans for as long as thirty minutes, to combine learned words in order to describe new situations or objects, to perceive difference and sameness, to understand 'if–then' concepts, to describe their moods, to lie, to select and use words in syntactical order, to express desire, to anticipate future events, to seek signed communication with others of their species and, in one extraordinary sequence (see below) to force the truth from a lying human.

Lana in pursuit of truth

Tim had entered the anteroom with a bowl of monkey chow. Lana had asked that it be loaded into the machine; however, the conditions of the test called for Tim not to comply, to load cabbage instead, and to declare that chow (which she had requested) was in the machine. Although Lana might have asked the machine to vend "chow", she did not—appropriate to the fact that cabbage, and not monkey chow, was in the vender.

She said:

Lana: Please machine give piece of cabbage. You (Tim) put chow in machine? (five times).

Tim (lying): Chow in machine. (In response to each of the five requests.)

Lana: Chow in machine?

Tim (still lying): Yes.

Lana: No chow in machine (which was true).

Tim: What in machine? (Repeated once.)

Lana: Cabbage in machine (which was true).

Tim: Yes, cabbage in machine.

Lana: You move cabbage out of machine.

Tim: Yes. (Whereupon he removed the cabbage and put in the monkey chow.)

Lana: Please machine give piece of chow. (Repeatedly until all was obtained.)'[30], [34], [35], [36]

In conclusion let us look once again at the ever-astounding honey bees and their methods of communication. The general story of the communication of the distance, the situation, and the direction of a food source by the dances of the returning worker bee on the vertical comb of the hive, has been known in general outline from the work of Karl von Frisch in the middle 1950s.

The basic correctness of the original conclusions has now been amply confirmed and established. But, far more than this, recent observations have shown overwhelmingly how adaptable, flexible, and 'purposive' is the use of these signs. For instance it has been argued that the use of the dances is rigidly controlled by the circumstances (such as the absence or presence of food). This is not so. For the dances most frequently used to signal the location of a food source are, under special conditions, also applied to other requirements of the mutually interdependent members of the colony of bees. After all, they are not *rigidly* used for foraging flights. When food is plentiful returning foragers often do not dance at all. The odours conveyed from one bee to another always help to direct recruits to new sources and often these alone are sufficient. Independent searching by individual foragers seems to be adequate under many conditions. Thus the dance-communication system is called into play primarily when the colony of bees is in great need of food; but it is not tightly linked to any one requirement; on the contrary it may be used for such different things as food, water, and resinous materials from plants (propolis). Moreover, when a colony of bees is engaged in swarming, the scouts search for cavities suitable to serve as the future home for the entire colony and report their location by the same dances —which are now performed when crawling over the mass of bees which makes up the swarm cluster.[31] When Lindauer observed the scouts of a swarm of bees which had moved only a short distance away from the original colony he found that the same marked bee would sometimes change her dance pattern from that indicating the location of a moderately suitable cavity to one signalling a better potential site for a new hive. This occurred after the dancer had received information from another bee and had flown out to inspect the superior cavity. Thus the same worker bee can be both a transmitter and receiver of information within a short period of time; and in spite of her motivation to dance about one location, she can also be influenced by the similar but more intense communication of another dancer. As Griffin[32] says,

'There is no escape from the conclusion that, in the special situation when swarming bees are in serious need of a new location in which the colony can continue its existence, the bees exchange information about the location and suitability of a potential hive site. Individual worker bees are swayed by this information to the extent that after inspection of alternative locations they change their preference and dance for the superior place rather than the one they first discovered. Only after many hours of such exchanges of information, involving dozens of bees, and only when the dances of virtually all the scouts indicate the same hive site, does the swarm as a whole fly off to it.' (Lindauer, 1971a). This consensus results from the communicative interactions between individual bees which alternatively 'speak' and 'listen'.

One of the philosophers (R. F. Terwilliger),[33] who argues specifically against the evidence from honey bees in his efforts to support his view of animals as Cartesian machines, says, 'No bee was ever seen dancing about yesterday's honey (he means of course *nectar*) not to mention tomorrow's. . . . Moreover bees never make mistakes in their dance.'

One of the many facts that Terwilliger, and other authors of a similar persuasion, ignore is that bees can be stimulated, by extreme food deficit, to dance during the middle of the night (a thing which they normally very rarely do) about a food source they have visited the day before, and will almost certainly visit again the next morning. In these circumstances a bee which has been dancing right up to sundown will, as soon as the morning comes, fly out to the same source, now, of course, *taking a very different direction relative to the sun, in its morning position.*

It is not so very surprising to find true linguistic ability in a primate with a brain construction so similar to that of ourselves. But it is indeed in a sense 'shocking' to find it in a bee where the neurons in the central nervous system can number hardly more than a few thousand.

REFERENCES

1. Hinde, R. A., *Animal Behaviour*, 2nd edn (New York: McGraw Hill, 1970).
2. Fentress, J. C., 'Dynamic boundaries of patterned behaviour: inter-action and self organization' in *Growing Points in Ethology* (edited by P. P. G. Bateson and R. A. Hinde) (Cambridge: CUP, 1976).

3. Hutchinson, J. B., *Advances in the Study of Behaviour*, 1976, **6,** 159–200.
4. Baerends, G. P. and Drent, O., *Behaviour Supplement* No. 17, 1970.
5. Huxley, J. S. (Editor), *Phil. Trans. R. Soc. Ser. B*, December 1976, **251,** 247–526.
6. Premack, D., *Psychol. Rev.*, 1959, **66,** 219–33.
7. Reese, E. S., 1963, referred to in Hinde, R. A., 1970, p. 333.
8. Bullock, T. H., 'The origins of patterned nervous discharge', *Behaviour*, 1961, **17,** 48–59.
9. Full references to these works may be found in Hinde, op. cit.
10. See Hinde, op. cit., pp. 410–11.
11. See also Huxley, J. S., 'Discussion of ritualisation behaviour in animals and men', *Phil. Trans. R. Soc. Lond.*, 1966, **251,** 247–526.
12. From Hinde, op. cit., pp. 64–5.
13. See Klopfer, P. H., *Behavioural Aspects of Ecology* (New Jersey: Prentice Hall, 1962).
14. Bower, T. C. R., *Animal Behaviour*, 1966, **14,** 395–8.
15. Barends, G. P. and Kruijt, J. P., 'Stimulus selection', in *Constraints on Learning: Limitations and predispositions*, edited by R. A. Hinde and J. Stevenson Hinde (New York: Academic Press, 1973), pp. 23–49.
16. See Goldman, O., 'Maturation of the mammalian nervous system and the ontogeny of behaviour', *Advances in the Study of Behaviour*, 1976, **7,** 1–90.
17. Bateson, P. P. G., 'Internal influences in early learning in birds', in *Constraints on Learning: Limitations and Predispositions*, edited by R. A. Hinde and J. Stevenson Hinde (New York: Academic Press, 1973), pp. 101–6, 108.
18. Thorpe, W. H., in *Non-Verbal Communication*, edited by R. A. Hinde (Cambridge: CUP, 1972), pp. 153–75.
19. Marler, P., and Mundinger, P., in the *Ontogeny of Vertebrate Behaviour*, edited by H. Moltz (New York: Academic Press, 1971), pp. 389–450.
20. See Bateson, P. P. G. and Hinde, R. A. (Editors), *Growing Points in Ethology* (Cambridge: CUP, 1976), p. 417.
21. For a general summary see Simmons, A. J., 'The sonar receiver of the Bat', in *Orientation: Sensory Basis*, edited by H. E. Adler, *Ann. N.Y. Acad. Sci.*, 1971, **188,** 161–74; Scales, G., and Pye, J. D., *Ultra Sonic Communication by Animals* (London: Chapman and Hall, 1974).
22. For further details on this fascinating topic see Simmonds, A. J., note 21.
23. See Thorpe, W. H., 'Vocal Communication in Birds', in *Non-Verbal Communication*, edited by R. A. Hinde (Cambridge: CUP, 1972), pp. 153–75.
24. Thorpe, W. H., and Hall-Craggs, J., in *Growing Points in Ethology*, edited by P. P. G. Bateson and R. A. Hinde (Cambridge: CUP, 1976), pp. 171–89.

25. Konishi, M., *Science*, 1969, **166**, 1178–81; *Nature*, 1969, **222**, 566.
26. Barlow, H. B., 'Simple units and sensation: a neuron doctrine for perceptual psychology?', *Perception*, 1972, **1**, 371–94.
27. Barlow, op. cit., p. 387.
28. See Zangwill, O. L., in *Current Problems in Animal Behaviour*, edited by W. H. Thorpe and O. L. Zangwill (Cambridge: CUP, 1961), pp. 59–86; 'Thought and the brain', *Brit. J. Psychol.*, 1976, **67**, 301–4.
29. Fabricius, E., 'Visual signals in animal behaviour', in *Biological Signals* (Lund, Sweden: Kingl. Fysiografiska Sallskapet, 1973), p. 122.
30. From Hayes, Harold T. P., 'The persuit of reason', *New York Times Magazine*, 12 June 1977. See also Rumbaugh, D. M., 1977.
31. Von Frisch, K., 1967; Lindauer, O., 1971.
32. Griffin, Donald R., *The Question of Animal Awareness: the evolutionary continuity of mental experience* (New York: Rockefeller University Press, 1976).
33. Terwilliger, R. F., *Meaning and Mind* (New York: Oxford Press, 1968). Hubel, D. H., and Wiesel, T. N., 'Receptive fields of single neurones in the cat's striate cortex', *J. Physiol.* (1959), **148**, pp. 572–80.
34. Rumbaugh, D. M. (Editor), *Language Learning by a Chimpanzee: The Lana Project* (New York: Academic Press, 1977).
35. Since the reports on this work with chimpanzees were published, studies have been proceeding with a gorilla (Koko) the preliminary results of which appear to provide even more striking evidence for cognition and language construction. After $2\frac{1}{2}$ years training Koko is said to have used 251 distinct signs within a single hour. See Patterson, F., 'The gestures of a gorilla: language acquisition in another pongoid species', in *Perspectives on Human Evolution, Vol. 5*, Hamburg, D., Goodall, J. and McCown, R. E. (eds.) (Menlo Park, Benjamin, 1978).
36. The recent response of an anthropologist to modern primate studies (Hill, J., *Ann Rev. Anthropology*, 1978, pp. 89–112) is of great interest. 'It is unlikely that any of us will in our lifetimes see again a scientific breakthrough as profound in its implications. . . .'

Postface: ethology—
what of the future?

We have seen that studies which clearly fit into the modern concept of ethology first took shape in France in the late eighteenth century, and in both France and England in the nineteenth century. These studies arose out of 'natural history' with its emphasis on the interest in the whole animal, in all its actions, in its natural environment and through all stages of its life. Because of this fundamental and all-embracing interest, ethologists paid attention firstly to the complete repertoire of actions and movements which the animal displayed—including of course its responses to changes in the environment, to the presence of other members of its own species and to other animals. So they naturally began to wonder (as mankind has always done) about the animal 'mind' and what it was that guided or drove animals to perform what, at first sight, often seemed curious or incomprehensible actions. This necessitated the accurate description of such remarkable events as the displays of the great bustard, of a mantis, or of the frilled lizard (*Chamydosaurus kingii*). The very description of these extraordinary pieces of behaviour inevitably led to speculation about their origins and their functions, and so, very early on, naturalists were interested in both function and causation; and the interest in these two aspects of behaviour give us the first and most obvious characteristics of the ethological approach. To this initial characterization of ethology were later added an interest in developmental and evolutionary explanations of behaviour. I believe one can say without doubt that the strength of ethology resides, and always has resided, first in its prime concentration on the behaviour of the animal as a whole and secondly on its fourfold approach to the subject. So ethology today has links, or roots, spreading out in four directions: (a) integrated neurophysiology and hormonal physiology; (b) behavioural ecology; (c) population biology; and (d) comparative psychology. In some ways, the last of these would seem to be the nearest in aim to ethology. Both are concerned primarily with the whole animal and its behaviour and both have links with physiology—there being in fact a whole branch of comparative psychology normally subsumed under a title of physiological psychology; which comes very close to the physiological interests of ethologists. Yet, strange to say, it is only relatively recently that comparative psychologists and ethologists have felt at home in each other's company. This is partly because of the ethologists' prime interest in causation and in the evolutionary aspects of the study—namely the selective pressures which have acted in limiting and controlling at almost every stage the development of natural behaviour.

The comparative psychologist on the other hand, historically and often individually, approached the study of behaviour from a very different viewpoint. Comparative psychology started from human psychology and is concerned with the nature and functioning of the human mind—briefly with 'human intelligence'—and so the comparative psychologist tended to consider animals primarily as beings of low intelligence, often minimal intelligence, compared with man. In fact it took a long time for many workers to realise that the word 'intelligence' by itself is of extraordinarily vague meaning—unless the circumstances under which the intelligence is supposed to manifest itself are made exactly clear. However I think there is no doubt that the links with integrative neurophysiology and hormonal physiology must remain, and will indeed be strengthened in the near future. Comparative psychology on the other hand, as the term has been used for the past fifty years or so, seems (temporarily one hopes) to have lost its identity and be on the wane.

Ethologists' links with behavioural ecology surely need to be strengthened; for I am sure that many ethologists have heretofore gravely neglected the ecological aspects of their subject. I believe that this tendency to expand and reach out on the ecological side will be very largely influenced, if not dominated, by population biology. As Macfarland remarked,[1] 'The recognition of competition as not the only way in which animals deploy their behavioural options, has led to a whole new method of analysing an animal's motivational properties, and has made it possible to formulate models in which animals can perform complex time-budgeting strategies, in which they can pursue more than one goal simultaneously.' This is to say, that not only are species-typical characteristics of behaviour subject to natural selection, but so also is the order and timing of their performance. 'Observational and ecological studies of an animal can be used to formulate a cost-function, representing the balance of costs and benefits of the various aspects of the behaviour of the animal.[2] The investigation of these features of order and timing in the field to the point at which theoretical predictions can be compared with observed behaviour sequences appears at present to be of formidable difficulty. But where such studies turn out to be practicable, to the point of securing results of sufficient rigour, it seems to me that a great future lies before them.

Recently we have heard a good deal about what is called 'sociobiology'—a quantitative study of the relations between the individuals and groups of social species of animals—as closely linked with the techniques of population biology. Social studies have, in recent years, developed very rapidly and provided results of great interest. This is particularly true of the study of primate biology and the social relationships of some apes and monkeys. I am sure this will continue and may be expected to provide results of increasing value and significance for ethology as a whole and also for our understanding of human behaviour. The ethology of social species is also likely, in my view, to prove extremely productive in relation to other social animals such as wolves, hunting dogs, antelopes, and a great many schooling fish—perhaps also whales and dolphins—but I fail to see any particular advantage in the grouping of subjects under 'sociobiology': a synthesis which seems to bracket population genetics, selection theory, socioecology, and ethology. This combination is attractive enough but I question the advantage of attempting to isolate the behaviour of what we call 'social' species from the 'non-social'. Animals are social in many different degrees for a great variety of reasons and in a great number of ways. The responses and the sensory equipment by which they maintain their sociality are by no means unique and can be found in different forms and different degrees of development throughout the animal kingdom.

Wilson looks forward to a future in which sociobiology and behavioural psychology, including population biology, have become a well-defined discipline apparently excluding ethology— which will then be left closely related to what he calls physiological psychology; in fact a rather tenuous bridge linking the two great developments, (a) integrative neurophysiology and (b) socio-biology. I see no signs or probability of this happening and if it did, it would, I believe, be a considerable disaster for biology. The ethological characteristics enunciated above have implications far beyond the social life of animals and it is obvious that the four ethological characteristics I have mentioned will not find a place in sociobiology as delimited by Wilson. To attempt to make them a kind of appendage to the study of sociobiology would, I believe, be disastrous and, fortunately, unlikely to succeed.

This is not intended to be a 'personal' attack and does not strike me as such. The view which I express is, I believe, one with which most European ethologists would agree. Wilson is the one who has put forward these predictions and they must be criticized. His own work on ants and other social insects is superb—as I think everyone will agree.

Wilson's approach is, in essence, reductionist; for he seems to believe that the characteristic study of whole patterns of animal behaviour will be eventually cannibalized by neurophysiology and sensory physiology from one end and by sociobiology and behavioural ecology from the other. I feel with C. W. Barlow (*Animal Behaviour*, vol. 24, p. 701, 1976) that the flow will be the other way, and that ecologists will become ethologists as population biology becomes increasingly reductionist. I think also, that while neurophysiology and cellular physiology have problems of enormous interest and promise in their own field, many such workers will see, as did von Holst, that large sections of their output become exposed to a new illumination as a result of the new understanding achieved by the ethological approach. I also therefore predict that many physiologists will also become ethologists as their science develops.

Ethology in my view is an integrative science, in many respects essential for the full and satisfactory development of all other disciplines which are concerned with the whole animal.

REFERENCES

1. Macfarland, D. J., *New Scientist*, 18 November 1976, 376–9.
2. Macfarland, D. J., in *Growing Points in Ethology*, edited by P. P. G. Bateson and R. A. Hinde (Cambridge: CUP, 1976).

Index

ABBOTT, T. K., 20
Adler, 28
Adlerz, 96
Adrian, 137
Aesop's *Fables*, 4
Albertus Magnus, St, 4
Aldrovandi, 4
Amberley, Lord, 19
Andrew, 137
anecdotal method, 25
Anrep, 28
appetitive behaviour, 39–40, 49, 98, 100, 102, 103, 105, 114, 123
Aristotle, 3, 45
Armstrong, E., 33–4, 136
Association for the Study of Animal Behaviour, 34, 72, 81, 117
automatism, 11, 12, 95
aversion, 39

BAERENDS, G., 113–15, 117, 128, 143
Bailey, S., 19
Baines, Prof., 19
Bannerman, Mrs D. A., 81
Barfield, 136
Barlow, C. W., 168
Barlow, H. B., 156, 157
Barrington, D., 18
Bateson, P. P. G., 149, 150
Beach, F. A., 124, 136
Beer, 56
behaviourism, 46, 50, 51, 56

Bekhterev, 51
Berkeley, Bishop, 19, 22
Bethe, 56, 94
Bewick, T., 18
Bingley, W., 25
bionomics, 3
Bol, 138
Books of Hours, 4
Boring, E. G., 25, 48
Bower, T. C. R., 143
Bühler, 41
Bullock, T. H., 133, 137
Bunsen, R., 55, 59
Butler, Bishop, 7

CARPENTER, C. R., 124
causation, x
Chamberlain, H. S., 55
Chapman, F., 76
Chauvin, R., 124
Chauvin-Muckensturm, 124
Chomsky, 159
competition, 167
conditioning, 28, 101, 118, 119
consciousness, 25, 38
consummatory acts, 100, 123, 129–32
Copernicus, 6
Couch, J., 25
Craig, W., 38–43, 48, 98
Cuvier, Baron G., 14–15, 16

d'ANGIVILLER, Mme, 10

Darchen, 124
Darwin, C., viii, ix, 5, 21, 24, 25, 33, 56, 94
Dawkins, R., 158
de Buffon, 12
de Haan, J. A. B., 73
displacement activity, 101, 104, 106, 129, 137–9
Doughty, 30
Drent, O., 128
drive, 100, 104, 105, 132–7, 139

ECOLOGY, 3, 16, 43, 114, 117, 166
Eibl-Eibesfeldt, I., 109
ethogram, 11
ethology, definition of, viii, 9, 16, 54
    early use of term, 43, 53, 67, 96
    future of, 165–9
    origin of word, 9
Exner, S., 64
expectancy, 41

FABRE, J.-H., 17, 43, 67, 96
Fabricius, E., 158
facilitation, 89
Fathers of the Church, 3
Fenton, 96
Fentress, J. C., 128, 136, 138
fixed action patterns, 100, 126–32, 139
Flourens, 15
Francis of Assisi, St, 4
Frederick II, 4
Frisch, K. von, 54, 59–66, 74, 113, 160

GALILEO, 6
Gall, F. J., 15
Gebhardt, Gretel, see Lorenz, Frau G.
Geoffroy-Saint-Hilaire, E., 14–16
Geoffroy-Saint-Hilaire, I., 16, 43
Gesner, 4
Giard, A., 16–17, 43, 53, 67
Gould, J. L., 65
Grassé, P.-P., 124
Gray, Sir James, 121, 122

Gray, P. H., 13, 19, 20, 21, 22, 23, 25
Griffin, D. R., 152, 161
Groos, K., 37

HABITUATION, 101
Haeckel, E., 3, 16
Haldane, J. B. S., 19
Hardy, Sir Alister, 116, 117
Hartmann, 37
Hassenstein, B., 82, 111
Hayes, H. T. P., 159
Hebb, 145
Hediger, H., 123, 125
Heinroth, O., 53–4, 67, 95, 96, 110, 123, 147
Helmholtz, 23
Henderson, L. J., 44
Hertwig, R. von, 62
Hertz, Mathilde, 74–5
Hess, K. von, 61–2
Hinde, R. A., 123, 128, 131, 133, 134, 135, 136, 138, 142, 152
Holst, E. von, 81–3, 106, 110–12, 138, 169
Howard, H. E., 29, 33–4, 117
Hubel, 155, 156
Hume, D., 14, 20
Huxley, J., 33–4, 117

IERSEL, J. van, 117, 138
imitation, 27
Imms, A. D., 75
imprinting, 24, 53, 99, 102, 122, 123, 147–50
inertia, 89
inheritance, 13, 14
inhibition, 89
instinct, ix, 18, 20, 23, 25, 26, 35–6, 39, 43, 47, 66, 68, 73, 87, 88, 94–106, 110, 111, 113, 114, 117, 119, 124, 133, 144–5
instinctive behaviour, 7, 47
intelligence, ix, 13, 20, 46, 103, 166
internal drive, 14

JAMES, W., 24, 37, 88
Jaynes, J., 14, 15

Jennings, H. S., 38

KINESIS, 90–1, 95, 98, 99, 105, 113
Kinsey, A. C., 45
Kirby, 37
Kirkman, F. B., 33, 34
Köhler, O., 77, 82, 112–13, 125
König, Frau L., 108–9
König, O., 108–9
Kortlandt, A., 74, 99, 104, 137
Kramer, G., 82
Kruijt, J. P., 143
Kuenen, D. J., 76
Kuhn, A., 89

LAMARCK, 13–14, 15
Lamarckism, 29
Lana (chimpanzee), 159–60
language learning, 158–60
Lashley, K. S., 39, 46–8, 49, 50, 51,
    68, 124, 157
latent learning, 102, 106
law of effect, 28
learning, 23, 98, 99, 101–2, 103,
    106, 119, 120, 145, 147–51
Lehrman, D., 125
Leroy, C. G., 10–13, 15, 16
Lewis, R. H., 24
Lindauer, O., 161
Lissmann, H., 58
Loeb, J., 37–8, 89, 94
Lorenz, Frau G., 69–70, 80, 81
Lorenz, K. Z., 42, 47, 49, 50, 54,
    66–71, 76–82, 95–9, 102–6,
    108, 109, 111, 112, 113, 119,
    122–3, 124, 131, 132, 139
Lucy (chimpanzee), 159

McBRIDE, E. W., 29
McDougall, W., 88
Macfarland, D. J., 167
Makkink, G. F., 73, 74
Marey, 55
Marler, P., 123
Marshall, F. H. A., 33–4
Martin, R., 110
Martina (pet goose), 70–1
Mason, W. A., 132

Massingham, H. J., 30
Matthews, G. V. T., 123
Metzger, W., 82
Mill, J. S., 9, 16
mimicry, 45
Mittelstaedt, H., 82, 111
Montague, T., 18
mood, 99
Morgan, L. H., 36
Morgan, Lloyd, 19, 24–30, 37, 50
Morgan's canon, 28
Müller, G. E., 95, 155

NATURAL SELECTION, viii, 16, 30, 45,
    167
nature versus nurture, 26
Nim (chimpanzee), 159
Nuremberg Naturalist, 10, 11

PAVLOV, 28, 51, 56, 79, 94
Pennant, T., 18
perception, 147, 151–7
Pernau, Baron von, 4
pheromones, 45
Portielje, A. F. J., 72–3
Premack, D., 132
Priestley, J. B., 81
problem solving, 20
psychology, vii–x, 9, 15, 25, 26,
    166, 168

RÄBER, H. R., 123
Raven, C., 5, 6
Ray, John, 4–8
reflexes, 88, 89, 95, 98, 106, 111
releasers, 23, 98, 101, 104, 105, 106,
    114, 129, 139–43, 147, 158
Richard, G., 124
Riley, Q., 76
Rilke, R. M., 55
ritualization, 129
Romanes, C. J., 21, 24, 25
Rumbaugh, D. M., 159
Russell, B., 19
Rymill, J., 76

SAINT PAUL, Ursula von, 82, 138
Sarah (chimpanzee), 159

Schenkel, R., 123
Schneirla, T. C., 125
Schoen, Laura, 82
Schopenhauer, 37
Selous, E., 30–3, 72, 117
Selous, F. C., 30
sensibility, 12
Sherrington, 89, 157
Skinner, 49
sociobiology, 167–8
social releaser, 101, 104
Spalding, D., 18–25, 26, 28, 53
specific action potential, 100
stimulus selection, 143–4
'superstition', 71
systematics, 5, 88

TAXES, 91–3, 95, 98, 99, 105, 113
taxonomy, 6, 54
Taylor, H. L., 44
Terwilliger, R. F., 162
Thompson, D'Arcy, 38
Thorndike, 26, 50
Thorpe, W. H., 119, 151
Tinbergen, N., 49, 54, 68, 74–7,
    80, 81, 82, 83, 99, 113, 115–18,
    122, 137
Tolman, 41
transformisme, 13, 14

trial and error, 13, 14, 102, 106
trophallaxis, 45
tropisms, 37

UEXKÜLL, J. von, 37, 54–9, 67, 110
Ulrich, 136

VERWEY, J., 74
vitalism, 54

WALLACE, A. R., 28
Washoe (chimpanzee), 159
Wasmann, E., 45
Watkins, G., 76
Watson, J. B., 24, 46, 51, 56
Wenner, A. M., 65
Wesley, J., 7
Wheeler, W. M., 43–5, 48, 68
White, Gilbert, 7, 18
Whitehead, A. N., 44
Whitman, C. O., 35, 39, 41, 43, 48
Wiesel, 155, 156
Willughby, 5, 6
Wilson, Edward, 168
Wodehouse, P. G., 123
Woodworth, 48
Wundt, 26

YERKES, R. M., 46